Men-at-Arms • 489

Lincoln's 90-Day Volunteers 1861

From Fort Sumter to First Bull Run

Ron Field • Illustrated by Adam Hook

Series editor Martin Windrow

First published in Great Britain in 2013 by Osprey Publishing, Midland House, West Way, Botley, Oxford, OX2 0PH, UK

44-02 23rd Street, Suite 219, Long Island City, NY 11101, USA

E-mail: info@ospreypublishing.com

OSPREY PUBLISHING IS PART OF THE OSPREY GROUP

A CIP catalog record for this book is available from the British Library

Print ISBN: 978 1 78096 918 3
PDF e-book ISBN: 978 1 78200 921 4
ePub e-book ISBN: 978 1 78200 920 7

Editor: Martin Windrow
Index by Alan Rutter
Typeset in Helvetica Neue and ITC New Baskerville
Originated by PDQ Media, Bungay, UK
Printed in China through Worldprint Ltd

13 14 15 16 17 18   10 9 8 7 6 5 4 3 2 1

Osprey Publishing is supporting the Woodland Trust, the UK's leading woodland conservation charity, by funding the dedication of trees.

www.ospreypublishing.com

Acknowledgments

The author wishes to thank the following for their generous assistance: Peter Harrington, Curator, Anne S.K. Brown Military Collection, Providence, Rhode Island; Maggie Marconi, Principal, Follett House Museum, Sandusky, Ohio; Erika Gorder, Special Collections and University Archives, Rutgers University Archives; Martha Mayo, Head, Center for Lowell History, University of Massachusetts Lowell; Kori Oberle, Director of the Hoard Historical Museum, and Karen O'Connor, Collections Curator, Fort Atkinson, Wisconsin; Clifton P. Hyatt, US Army Heritage and Education Center; Michael J. McAfee; Daniel Miller; Don Troiani; Paul Mehney; Brad and Donna Pruden; Allen Cebula; Dr Steven Altic; Ron Swanson, Marius Peladeau and Jonathan Soffe.

Artist's Note

Readers may care to note that the original paintings from which the color plates in this book were prepared are available for private sale. All reproduction copyright whatsoever is retained by the Publishers. All enquiries should be addressed to:

Scorpio Paintings, 158 Mill Road, Hailsham, East Sussex BN27 2SH, UK
scorpiopaintings@btinternet.com

The Publishers regret that they can enter into no correspondence upon this matter.

Editor's Note

Since period spellings have been preserved in verbatim quotations, there are inevitable inconsistencies between these and the body text, e.g. "grey/ gray".

LINCOLN'S 90-DAY VOLUNTEERS 1861

THE CALL TO ARMS

Having enrolled in the Lowell City Guard, 6th Massachusetts Volunteer Militia on January 21, 1861, Luther Ladd was killed by the pro-secessionist mob as his regiment passed through Baltimore on April 19. According to a contemporary account, he was shot in the thigh and "bled to death at once." He wears the full-dress uniform still used by the 6th Massachusetts after its reorganization from the 5th Regiment of Light Infantry, MVM, in 1855. This consisted of an 1851-pattern cap with pompon, a dark blue coatee with white trim and fringed epaulets, and light blue trousers. Characteristic of Massachusetts volunteers, his waist belt is black while his shoulder belt is whitened buff leather. (Lowell Historical Society)

On April 15, 1861, Abraham Lincoln, the only recently inaugurated President of the United States, issued "a Call to Arms" following the bombardment of Fort Sumter in Charleston Harbor, South Carolina, and its surrender to troops representing the seven seceded Confederate States of the lower South. In anticipation of a short conflict, the president asked the loyal northern and border states for 75,000 militiamen for just 90 days' service to put down the rebellion.[1] Lincoln made this request under an act of Congress dated February 28, 1795, for "calling out the militia to execute the laws of the Union, to suppress insurrection, [and] to repel invasion." His call was rendered necessary by the fact that at the outbreak of war the regular US Army numbered only 16,367 officers and men in widely dispersed units, the majority in coastal forts or on the distant Western frontier, while by April 15 the Confederate States already had some 35,000 men under arms. The initial quota of troops required from each state was as follows:

Pennsylvania: 16 regiments, subsequently reduced to 14, then increased to 25; New York: 11 regiments (one of which served for only 30 days); Ohio: 13 regiments; Indiana and Illinois: 6 regiments each; New Jersey: 4 regiments; Connecticut: 3 regiments; Massachusetts: 2 regiments, increased to 5, plus one battalion and a battery; Maine, New Hampshire, Vermont, Rhode Island, Delaware, Michigan, Wisconsin, and Iowa: a single regiment each.

Although not included in the Presidential call, Minnesota also offered one regiment, which was accepted. The border "slave states" of Maryland, Kentucky, Missouri, plus the upper slave states of Arkansas, North Carolina, Tennessee, and Virginia – which at that date had not yet decided on secession – also received requisitions for troops, but failed to comply.

Each of the regiments received into Federal service was to be of infantry or riflemen; although no cavalry were required, one Pennsylvania troop was offered and accepted. As originally ordered, each of these regiments, assembled from smaller volunteer units, was to consist of an aggregate of 780 officers and men organized into ten companies. The total to be called out was thus 73,391. The remainder was made up by the militia of the District of Columbia, which actually furnished 4,720 men. In addition, western Virginia and Kansas supplied 900 and 650 men respectively, making a grand total of 91,816 of these 90-day volunteers.

---

1   The initial call for the mobilization of volunteers in the South was rather more realistic; both six-month and twelve-month terms of service were authorized by the Confederate States Congress on March 6, 1861. For categories of Confederate militia and volunteers, see MAA 423, *The Confederate Army 1861–65 (1): South Carolina & Mississippi*, page 4.

CHRONOLOGY

November 1860	Abraham Lincoln wins presidential election.
December 20 1861	South Carolina secedes from the Union.
January–April	Secession of Mississippi, Florida, Alabama, Georgia, Louisiana, and Texas.
February 8–9	Provisional Confederate States government is established, and elects Jefferson Davis as president. Widespread seizure of US military facilities in South.
March 4	Inauguration of President Lincoln.
March 6	President Davis calls for 100,000 Confederate volunteers for 6 or 12 months' service.
April 12–14	Fighting begins with bombardment of Fort Sumter by South Carolina forces under BrigGen Pierre G.T. Beauregard; Federal garrison surrenders.
April 15	President Lincoln calls for volunteers for 3 months' service.
April 17–May 24	Virginia secedes, followed by Arkansas, Tennessee, and North Carolina, and Kentucky declares its neutrality.
April 19	President Lincoln declares blockade of Confederate ports.
May 24	Virginia militia occupy Alexandria area, and establish batteries controlling Potomac River approaches to Washington, DC.
July 2	Lincoln calls for 300,000 volunteers for three years' service.
June–July Operations in Virginia	Both sides assemble motley armies of ill-trained and often inadequately officered troops between the two capitals – Washington, DC, and Richmond, VA. Brigadier General Irvin McDowell commands the Union Army of Northeastern Virginia (later, "of the Potomac"). Beauregard emplaces Confederate troops around strategic rail hub of Manassas Junction south of Bull Run River.

Western Virginia campaign: Leading Ohio volunteers, Union MajGen George B. McClellan clears western Virginia; actions at Philippi (June 3) and Rich Mountain/ Carrick's Ford (July 17).

Eastern Virginia: Skirmish at Big Bethel near Union-held Fortress Monroe (June 10).

Shenandoah Valley campaign, northern Virginia: Confederate commander BrigGen Joseph E. Johnston, with Col Thomas J. Jackson leading one of his brigades, outmaneuvers the hesitant Union commander BrigGen Robert Patterson.

First Bull Run (Manassas) campaign: Prompted by Northern political clamor for an advance on Richmond, and the imminent end of his volunteers' 90-day term of service, McDowell advances toward Manassas Junction (July 16). Johnston's Confederate corps slips away from BrigGen Patterson's surveillance in the Shenandoah Valley and hurries east, arriving to

Photographed wearing full dress in camp in 1860, the 7th New York State Militia was one of the first regiments to rush to the defense of the Federal capital in April 1861, having received a special call from President Abraham Lincoln. (Author's collection)

link with Beauregard at Manassas from July 20. On July 21, McDowell – with only two experienced US regular battalions among his 28,500 troops deployed – makes piecemeal attacks, and attempts a right-flanking maneuver for which his staff and troops are insufficiently trained. The attack is checked by Jackson's speedy movement, and by his Virginian brigade "standing like a stone wall." The Union army flees in confusion, covered by rearguard actions by MajGen George Sykes's regular infantry and Maj Innis Palmer's regular cavalry battalions.[2] Union casualties are some 2,700, and would have been greater had President Davis authorized a pursuit; the Confederates suffer about 1,980 casualties.

Service of 90-Day Volunteers, 1861

Pennsylvania
Patterson's Virginia campaign: Cavalry Troop, 1st–3rd Regts; 6th–17th; 20th; 21st; 23rd; 24th; 25th (and at Washington, DC)
Alexandria, Virginia: 4th, 5th
New York
Garrison duty at/near Washington, DC: 5th (also Patterson's VA campaign); 6th (and guard duty in Maryland); 7th (30 days only); 12th (also Patterson's VA campaign); 25th; 28th
Guard duty in Maryland: 6th (and at Washington, DC); 13th; 20th
First Bull Run campaign: 8th; 69th; 71st
Ohio
Western Virginia campaign: 14th–23rd
First Bull Run campaign: 1st; 2nd
Indiana
Western Virginia campaign: 6th–10th; 11th (and guard duty in Maryland)
Illinois
Garrison duty, Illinois: 7th (Cairo and Mound City; and at St Louis, MO); 8th (Cairo); 9th; 10th; 11th (and at Bird Point, MO); 12th
New Jersey
First Bull Run campaign (uncommitted reserves): 1st–4th

Massachusetts
Garrison duty at Fortress Monroe, VA: 3rd; 4th (and Big Bethel campaign)
First Bull Run campaign: 5th
Guard duty: 6th (Baltimore and Relay House, MD); 8th (Washington, DC, and Relay House); 3rd Bn (Annapolis and Baltimore); Artillery (Annapolis and Relay House)
Maine Garrison duty at Washington, DC: 1st
New Hampshire Patterson's Virginia campaign: 1st
Vermont Big Bethel campaign, and garrison duty Fortress Monroe, VA: 1st
Rhode Island First Bull Run campaign: 1st
Connecticut First Bull Run campaign: 1st–3rd
Delaware Guard duty in Maryland: 1st
Michigan First Bull Run campaign: 1st
Wisconsin Patterson's Virginia campaign: 1st
Iowa Wilson's Creek campaign, Missouri (August): 1st
District of Columbia Garrison duty, Washington, DC: 8 battalions

Union infantry at First Bull Run (First Manassas), July 21, 1861

First Division (Tyler):
1st Brigade (Keyes)
1st–3rd Connecticut (all*), 2nd Maine (***)
2nd Bde (Schenck)
2nd New York (***), 1st & 2nd Ohio (both*)
3rd Bde (Sherman)
13th, 69th, & 79th New York (all*), 2nd Wisconsin (***)
4th Bde (Richardson)
1st Massachusetts (***), 2nd & 3rd Michigan (both***), 12th New York (*)
Second Div (Hunter):
1st Bde (Porter)
14th & 27th New York (both***), US Infantry Bn, US Marine Bn
2nd Bde (Burnside)
2nd New Hampshire, (***), 71st New York (*), 1st Rhode Island (*). 2nd Rhode Island (***)

Third Div (Heintzelman):
1st Bde (Franklin)
5th Massachusetts (*), 11th Massachusetts (***), 1st Minnesota (*** from May 10)
2nd Bde (Wilcox)
1st Michigan (*), 4th Michigan, 11th & 38th New York (all***)
3rd Bde (Howard)
3rd, 4th & 5th Maine, 2nd Vermont (all***)
Fourth (Reserve) Div (Runyon):
No brigade organization
1st–4th New Jersey (all*), 41st New York (all***),
Fifth Div (Miles):
1st Bde (Blenker)
8th New York (**), 29th, & 39th New York, 27th Pennsylvania (all***)
2nd Bde (Davies)
16th, 18th, 31st, & 32nd New York (all***)

Note: Includes units raised for, or converted to, terms over 90 days.
* = 90-day unit; **= 2-year unit; ***=3-year unit.

2   The US Infantry Battalion comprised Cos C & K, 2nd US Inf Regt; Cos B, D, G, H & K, 3rd US Inf; and Co G, 8th US Infantry. Serving with it in Gen Porter's 1st Brigade of Gen Hunter's Second Division was the US Cavalry Bn, comprising Cos A & E, 1st US Cav Regt; Cos B, E, G & I, 2nd US Cav; and Co K, 2nd US Dragoons. The US Marine Bn which also served in this brigade was almost entirely composed of new recruits, so was not comparable to these two units in terms of experience.

UNITS, UNIFORMS, & EQUIPMENT

A Pennsylvania rifle company formed in 1858, the Sarsfield Rifles became part of the Rifle Battalion of Philadelphia. Unusually, the "hunting shirt"-style coat worn by this enlisted man has a 2in-long fringe around the skirts (see Plate A1). The Philadelphia Rifle Battalion was expanded into the German Rifle Regiment or 21st Pennsylvania Infantry for three months' service in April 1861. (Author's collection)

PENNSYLVANIA

The Commonwealth of Pennsylvania was required to provide 16 regiments, although this was reduced to 14 several days later. Those accepted consisted of the eight Philadelphia regiments, while separate militia companies were recruited throughout the state. As the authorities were concerned about the condition of these volunteers, amounting to over 400 companies, permission was granted for the raising of new units. As a result, a total of 25 regiments were actually recruited, and the Federal government was induced to accept them all. Those from Philadelphia consisted of the 17th through 24th Infantry, while those organized elsewhere throughout the state were the 1st through 16th and 25th regiments.

The first State troops to reach Washington, DC, following Lincoln's initial call were from Pennsylvania. During the early hours of April 18, five companies amounting to 530 men – composed of the Ringgold Light Artillery, Logan Guards, Allen Rifles, Washington Artillery, and National Light Infantry – arrived in the city. In the capital, the *National Republican* of April 19 reported: "Some of the men say that they came off in such haste that they did not take time to prepare for the journey, but came off in their working clothes from their places of business." Only the Logan Guards, amounting to 34 men, carried Springfield muskets, and these were without ammunition; however, one man carried a box of percussion caps, which he distributed amongst his comrades. Hence, with muskets capped and carried half-cocked at "support arms," they had fooled the pro-Confederate mob into thinking their weapons were loaded while the militiamen passed unmolested through pro-secessionist Baltimore, Maryland. The arrival of these troops caused great rejoicing in the capital, and gained for them the title of "The First Defenders." These companies eventually entered three months' service as part of the 25th Pennsylvania.

Many of the companies forming the three-month regiments from this state wore prewar full-dress or fatigue uniforms. As the only cavalry unit accepted at this stage in the war, the wealthy First Troop, Philadelphia City Cavalry provided their own service uniforms, plus horses and equipments, which cost between $300 and $500 per man. Other companies, such as the Philadelphia Zouaves and the National Guards, also wore distinctive uniforms.

Uniform procurement

In order to prepare for war, Pennsylvania set about clothing its volunteers in uniforms based on Federal regulations. With the reorganization of the State Military Establishment on April 12, Reuben C. Hale was appointed Quartermaster-General. Challenged with the task of finding uniforms for the flood of volunteers, Governor Andrew Curtin sent state agent Robert Martin, with Capt George Gibson of the US Army, to Philadelphia to purchase cloth. By April 23, Martin had established a "uniform manufactory" at the Girard House, a recently vacated hotel off Market Street in that city. Four days later the Philadelphia press was able to report that about 23,000 garments had been produced by 30 cutters and 525 females employed in sewing.

Probably referring to the city regiments, the *Philadelphia Inquirer* of April 30 stated: "Most of the volunteers who are about starting South have been furnished with the new regulation garments." By the month's end the same journal commented that "The State order for 10,000 suits of clothing, is rapidly approaching completion... Some of the garments are entirely finished, and most of the hands are now busy on sack coats and overcoats." According to the *Daily Patriot* of Harrisburg, dated April 23, the uniforms being made were "neat, serviceable, becoming, and exceedingly comfortable. Blue sack coats loose and easy to the form; blue pantaloons cut large and free, gray flannel shirts, open at the neck, and fatigue caps," which contrasted "favorably with the tight padded coats, leather stocks and hats, shakos, &c., of other times."

Several weeks later the volunteers began to receive uniforms. Those at Camp Slifer, Chambersburg, were in possession of some contract clothing by May 9, as two days later the *Philadelphia Inquirer* reported that all the companies composing the 7th, 8th, and 10th Pennsylvania had received their "blouse, pants and gray shirts." The 2nd Pennsylvania at Camp Scott, York, received its issue on May 13; according to a letter published in the *Columbia Spy* on May 18, this consisted of a "blue blouse (coarse in material and make), gray trousers, blue cap and gray overcoat."

Complaints soon began to be heard about the poor quality of uniforms. A letter in the *Pittsburgh Gazette* on May 29 from an enlisted man in the 12th Pennsylvania stated: "Of the clothing furnished us lately... Our blouses are of every shade, dark and light blue, dark and light gray – they are the only serviceable articles of clothing we have received, and they are dear at a dollar and a half. I would not give a farmer's 'wamus' for two of them." Regarding the pants, the correspondent complained that they "gave way the first time I stooped, the waist or body band going up with the suspenders, the seat and legs dropping down." Some inferior headgear also appears to have been produced; on May 30, the *Philadelphia Inquirer* advised that the caps furnished the 1st Pennsylvania were "scarcely a hue of their original color. The blue has entirely deserted them, and they now have the foxy red appearance which common blue cloth colored with logwood assumes after a few days exposure to wind and rain."

The poor state of clothing at the capital came to the attention of Governor Curtin, who immediately dispatched Benjamin Haywood, a "prominent citizen of Schuylkill county," to observe the condition of the Pennsylvania regiments. By May 28, Haywood reported that the 25th Pennsylvania quartered at the Arsenal were "not badly off," having received Federal-issue uniforms via a directive originally issued by Secretary of War Simon Cameron on April 23. However, the 4th and 5th Pennsylvania were found to be "suffering greatly" with blouses and pants of "all colors, and made of damaged goods of inferior quality, mostly of 'shoddy' and some of 'Kentucky jean.'"

As late as July 19, the 19th Pennsylvania paraded in Baltimore "still clad in the miserable dirty gray, old pantaloons and roundabouts...". According to the *Philadelphia Inquirer*, "Quite a number of facetious fellows... by way of practically demonstrating the swindle practiced

Organized into a regiment of eight companies in 1860, the National Guards of Philadelphia had adopted a new uniform in February 1859, which consisted of a gray tail coat with black and gold trim including fringed epaulets, matching trousers with a broad black stripe, and a black dress cap with black pompon. Note the chevrons-and-diamond of this first sergeant. This regiment tendered its services to the Federal government on April 16, 1861, and served for three months as the 19th Pennsylvania Infantry. (Anne S.K. Brown Military Collection)

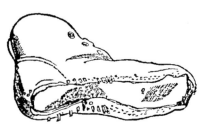

Entitled "Pair of Pantaloons after Four Days' Wear at Camp Scott," and "A White-Pine Sole Army Shoe, after Three Days' Wear," these engravings were published in the *Philadelphia Inquirer* on May 21, 1861 to expose the "barefaced robbery" of the military suppliers providing clothing and footwear for the troops at Camp Scott, near York, Pennsylvania. (Author's collection)

upon them, had immense red patches conspicuously displayed on portions of their garments. When drawn up in line these scarlet appendages looked remarkably funny, and told more forcibly than language how shamefully those exhibiting them had been cheated."

Indictment of profiteers

Much of the inferior clothing produced at the Girard House factory in Philadelphia was the result of a contract issued by Charles "Bucky" Neal, a lawyer and "special agent" of Governor Curtin, to Frowenfeld & Morganstern, a group of Pittsburgh businessmen, for $22,385-worth of uniforms to be made from cloth purchased in Philadelphia. On June 16 this firm plus "Bucky" Neal were indicted for fraud in furnishing inferior clothing to the Commonwealth. Preliminary proceedings were held on July 2; the case against them finally came before the Criminal Court in Pittsburgh on April 2, 1862, when the Morganstern brothers and two of the Frowenfeld brothers were "ready and anxious to have their case disposed of." As Emanuel and Maurice Frowenfeld, plus "Bucky" Neal, were absent and "supposed to be in Europe," Judge Thomas Mellon stated that "the parties who had fled to avoid a trial should be presumed dishonest," while those who presented themselves in court were acquitted, being adjudged in the *Pittsburgh Gazette* of April 3, 1862 to have "borne up manfully under a tremendous pressure of public opinion."

Meanwhile, by May 23, 1861, the Quartermaster-General's office at Harrisburg had issued further contracts to reclothe about 15,000 volunteers, requesting "Indigo blue flannel blouses," "Blue Army Cloth Trousers," "Blue Cloth Caps, Army Regulation," and "Light Blue Army Cloth Overcoats." As a result, new uniforms were issued to the 4th and 5th Pennsylvania, which were "in actual service and in great need of proper clothing." Both of these regiments had been assigned to the 1st Brigade, Third Division, Army of Northeastern Virginia. On June 15, the 5th Pennsylvania was inspected at Alexandria, VA, and the *Philadelphia Inquirer* reported on the changed appearance of the regiment, stating that it was difficult to believe they were "the same men who were formerly designated as the 'Ragged Fifth.' " On June 16, a member of the Eagle Guards (Co H, 4th Pennsylvania), encamped outside Washington, wrote a letter to the *Central Press* of Bellefonte, Pennsylvania, stating: "The old 'uniforms' furnished us by the State in the first instance have been replaced by others of a substantial nature, together with cartouche-boxes, knapsacks, provision sacks, canteens, &c."

NEW YORK

The Empire State provided 11 militia regiments totaling 8,450 men. These consisted of the 5th through 8th, 12th, 13th, 28th, 69th, and 71st regiments from New York and Brooklyn, the 20th from Kingston, and the 25th from Albany. All left the state for Washington, DC, Annapolis, MD, or Fortress Monroe, VA, between April 19 and 27, 1861. As a result of a thriving militia system, the New York volunteers were mostly well-uniformed.

The 5th through 8th New York State Militia

Composed principally of Germans from New York City, the 5th New York State Militia (NYSM), or Jefferson Guard, wore "dark gray pants, dark blue coats and caps, and army overcoats" when they sailed for Fortress Monroe on April 27, according to the *New York Herald*. The 6th NYSM, or Governor's Guard, left for Washington, DC, on April 21 wearing "the dress cap and pompon, the uniform frock coat and overcoat, and pants" based on New York State dress regulations of 1858. Essentially the uniform adopted by the US Army in 1854, this was composed of a dark blue frock coat and sky-blue pants with an 1854-pattern dress cap. Fatigue jackets were packed in knapsacks. Much of this clothing was soon replaced by jackets, trousers, hats and overcoats supplied by the state.

Departing New York on April 19 as the result of a special call from President Lincoln, the elite 7th NYSM was mustered into service for only 30 days on arrival at the Federal capital a week later. According to the *New York Times*, this regiment left wearing a "full fatigue dress" consisting of a "gray uniform, with black trimmings" plus "gray cap and long blue overcoats." During their stay in the capital the 7th NYSM received a supply of "loose, dark gray, knit worsted jackets" called "Aspinwalls" after their donor, retired businessman William Aspinwall. This garment made a marked change in the appearance of the regiment, as one militiaman wrote in the regimental history: "No more tight-bodied dress-coats; no more pretty white cross-belts to hamper us down; no more heavy, stiff caps; no more fashionable pantaloons. Give us a little time after we get home – if we do get there – and we will show you a serviceable, neat, and inexpensive uniform."

Known as the Washington Greys, the 8th NYSM was reported in the *Evening Star* of Washington, DC, on May 18 to be wearing a uniform "the same as the New York Seventh." Some of the 8th NYSM were photographed on July 17 in camp at Fairfax Courthouse, VA, prior to the Bull Run campaign, wearing four-button gray sack coats issued to new recruits by the state quartermaster department before departure for the front.

In "marching order" and wearing "full fatigue," this enlisted man of 3rd Company, 7th New York State Militia is uniformed in gray trimmed with black, and armed with the Model 1855 musket received by the regiment in 1858. He is equipped with a militia box-knapsack topped with a blanket roll, a cartridge box and bayonet scabbard suspended from whitened buff leather shoulder belts, a cap pouch and a canteen. (USAMHI)

Encamped at Arlington, Virginia, during June 1861, some of these volunteers of the 8th NYSM wear the gray four-button sack coats issued before departure for the front. The man lying at front left is showing off the militia box-knapsack, with a mess tin in its black oilskin cover attached. Note the two African American servants standing at the left. The man at right is seated on a barrel labeled "W.G." and "8th Regt." (Library of Congress LC-USZ62-48411)

This unidentified sergeant of Co B, 13th NYSM, has a "Union Cockade" pinned to his breast in this photograph taken in Baltimore; he wears the 1857-pattern fatigue uniform regulated before this company adopted zouave dress in the second half of 1860. He carries a non-regulation militia officer's sword with Roman helmet pommel in a dark leather frog attached to his belt, the weight of which is supported by a leather belt loop sewn to the waist of his jacket. Note the black jacket trim including cuff patches and chevrons, and the very full cut of the pants. (Michael J. McAfee Collection)

The 12th, 13th, 28th, 69th, & 71st NYSM

According to the *National Republican* of April 28, the 400-strong nucleus of the 12th NYSM, or Independence Guard, arrived in the Federal capital wearing the uniform adopted by the regiment in 1857: "a dark blue frock coat, trimmed with light blue; blue pantaloons, with a white stripe; and the army regulation cap." The 12th received a new regimental uniform on May 9 after its arrival. The *New York Herald* commented that it was "styled the *Chasseur d'Affrique* [*sic*], is something like the Zouave costume, and will also be provided for the volunteers, as well as for the regular members of the regiment." According to the *Evening Star* of May 10, this consisted of a "bright blue fatigue cap trimmed with white cord, short chasseur coat with slashed skirt, the material being of dark blue set off at the seams with white [actually light blue] cord." The pants were "wide Zouave of light grayish blue, made to buckle around the ankle under high Zouave leggings." The 12th NYSM was the first Union regiment to advance into Virginia when it crossed the Long Bridge over the Potomac on May 23.

Organized in Brooklyn, the 13th NYSM, also known as the National Greys, wore the fatigue uniform detailed in their "Bill of Dress" adopted in 1857, which required a fatigue jacket of "cadet mixed gray cloth, the same color and shade as used at West Point," with black mohair binding around the collar, black shoulder straps and cuff patches. Trousers were also gray with black seam stripes. Gray caps had a black band and a "gilt block number 13," above which was pinned the company letter. Overcoats were sky-blue. Impressed by the appearance of the Chicago Zouave Cadets during their visit to Brooklyn in July 1860, Co B of the 13th NYSM adopted a zouave uniform. This regiment performed garrison duty at Annapolis, guarding railroads until it was moved to Baltimore in June. The only action it saw was the capture of a Confederate-held armory in Easton, MD, on May 18; this surrendered without a fight, although one New Yorker was supposedly killed.

Also organized in Brooklyn and composed mainly of Germans, the 28th NYSM spent most of their time in the Washington defenses, guarding the bridge at Georgetown during the battle at Bull Run on July 21. On the return of this regiment to New York seven days later, the *New York Herald* reported that the "men looked exceedingly well by the light of the street lamps, in their gray uniforms, which were not so much soiled as those of the men who had been in actual conflict."

Classed as "Artillery doing duty as Light Infantry" in prewar years, the 69th NYSM, or National Cadets, wore a uniform patterned on that prescribed by the New York State dress regulations of 1858. For fatigue purposes, this consisted of a dark blue frock coat with red trim and shoulder straps, sky-blue trousers with red seam stripes, and a dark blue forage cap. Recruits unable to acquire this uniform complete appear to have been supplied with flannel shirts and dark blue New York State artillery-pattern fatigue jackets. Joining the 69th NYSM as Co K on May 23, the Irish Zouaves were reported by a *New York Herald* correspondent to be wearing "a loose navy blue jacket fringed with red, and pantaloons of a bluish gray, with caps *a la* Sixty-ninth regiment." On arrival in

Washington, DC, they were further described by the *National Republican* as being uniformed in "a dark-blue Zouave jacket, gray Zouave pants, all trimmed with red, and blue Zouave cap" (see photograph, page 44). Upon return to New York City on July 26 following hard fighting at Bull Run, the whole regiment was described by the *New York Herald* as "woefully in want of clothing. The men were dressed in anything but the uniform of the Sixty-ninth. Southern and Northern uniforms were in their ranks, but, dressed as they were, they were the Sixty-ninth still, and New York recognized and welcomed them in their disguise."

Formed among the American-born citizens of New York City in the early 1850s, the 71st NYSM or American Guard departed for Washington, DC, on April 20 dressed in "full fatigue, with fatigue cap," consisting of "dark blue suits trimmed with black and gold, and blue overcoats." This was further reported in the *National Republican* on April 29, as being a "dark-blue coat, blue pants with black stripe and gilt borders, and blue fatigue cap." The *New York Herald* stated that recruits lacking a uniform were "dressed as taste and fancy dictated, and presented a most motley appearance." According to the regimental history, when the 71st NYSM marched out of the Navy Yard to join Ambrose Burnside's brigade prior to Bull Run on July 16 its coats had been exchanged for "a gray blouse."

According to Enos B. Vail, new recruits for the 20th NYSM, or Ulster Guard, were given a fatigue uniform consisting of "a soft, light colored Kossuth hat, and a leather collar [or stock] about two inches high." After arrival at Annapolis Junction on May 8, the Ulster Guard was described as consisting of "countrymen from the interior counties of the State" who wore "a blue-black frock coat, gray pants, and a dull white felt hat, now so discolored that it would pass for brown, upon which is penciled in charcoal, 'Twentieth regiment.' "

Also organized at Albany, the 25th NYSM wore gray frock coats trimmed with red, medium blue pants with white seam stripes, and blue forage caps. Mustered-in on April 23, the elite Albany Burgess Corps (Co R of this regiment) was provided with "two full uniforms [including dark blue frock coats]." On return to Albany on July 28 after service in the Washington defenses, the regiment was reported by the *New York Herald* as "tough and well, but much dilapidated as to clothing."

OHIO

The 1st & 2nd Ohio Volunteer Infantry

When Governor William Dennison, Jr, issued a call for volunteers, 20 companies offered their services, while countless other units were recruited all over Ohio. By April 19 some of these troops had been organized into the 1st and 2nd Ohio Volunteer Infantry, while others would form another 11 regiments. Informed that they would be uniformed by the Federal government, the first two regiments left for the front with many men wearing civilian clothing. Some companies may have fitted themselves out in a uniform based on the General Regulations adopted by Ohio in 1859, which was patterned after that of the US Army but with a sky-blue jacket for fatigue. The progress east of these regiments was temporarily halted at Lancaster, PA, by news of the burning of the bridges on the North Central Railroad and the pro-secessionist riots in Baltimore,

Mustering into Federal service in April 1861 as a private in the 13th Regiment, NYSM, George W. Scott is seen here wearing the zouave uniform adopted by Co B in 1860 in imitation of a Chicago unit (see Plate B2). His belt plate bears the company letter "B" plus "National/Greys," and his waist belt supports a non-regulation pattern cap pouch. (Anne S.K. Brown Military Collection)

A nurseryman in Fairfield, Ohio, when he enlisted in Co A, 1st Ohio Infantry, the 18-year-old Benjamin F. Coffman probably wears the Federal-style uniform issued to his regiment by the beginning of June 1861. Note the company letter, and the regimental number in the curl of the infantry buglehorn badge on his forage cap. (Dr Stephen Altic Collection)

Seated on a packing box labeled "Camp Dennison," this enlisted man of the Tyler Guard (Co G, 17th Ohio Infantry) wears a uniform closely conforming to Federal regulations, although the contractor has added piping on the cap and trousers. Note the shoulder scales, which were usually reserved for full dress. His revolver and knife may be simply photographer's props, although early-war volunteers often carried such personal sidearms until orders were issued to discard them. (Brad & Donna Pruden Collection)

and new orders were received to purchase uniforms from the Pennsylvania state clothing establishment.

In a letter published in the *Cleveland Plain Dealer* dated May 3, a member of the Cleveland Greys (Co E, 1st Ohio) wrote: "We have not yet been uniformed, but probably will be tomorrow or next day. We have received shirts (red woollen), shoes, hats and haversacks, in which to carry provisions while on the march, and expect to use the latter very soon." When no clear date for delivery of uniforms via Pennsylvania could be confirmed, Ohio agent James M. Brown was authorized to independently purchase cloth and contract for making the uniforms. By May 15, Brown reported that 1,720 suits had been supplied to the 1st and 2nd Ohio, consisting of "one black felt hat and ornaments, one black pilot cloth overcoat, one blue flannel blouse… one pair pantaloons … [and] one pair brogan shoes." On May 19, Pvt G. Chase of the Zanesville Guards (Co H, 1st Ohio) wrote to the *Daily Zanesville Courier* from Camp McClelland, PA, describing this as consisting of "Cheap felt hats the remains of old stock of numerous patterns, a *coarse* blue Blouse of Dark Flannel, coarse gray pants of inferior quality, which have already commenced to wear out and will be gone in 6 weeks, 2 red flannel shirts, 1 blanket, 1 pair brogans, a coarse overcoat – all of these are of the poorest quality…." Two days later, a letter published in the *Cincinnati Daily Commercial* from an unknown Ohio volunteer at the same encampment stated: "We have received our uniform: it is of the 'bob-tail' species… They will not last long; they are about wore out."

In a letter dated June 2 written to Governor Dennison from Willard's Hotel in Washington, DC, *aide de camp* Maj R. Corwine wrote that the 1st and 2nd Ohio were in a "most deplorable" condition. Some were literally in rags, and were called the "pauper" regiments by the citizens of Washington. Corwine assured the Ohio volunteers that their state governor had no knowledge of their true condition, and that Dennison had regarded them as exclusively under the jurisdiction of the Federal government from the moment it took charge of the regiments.

By June 6, state agent and Cincinnati businessman William Platt had been sent to Washington to investigate, and found the 1st Ohio in receipt of Federal-issue uniforms as a result of the directive originally issued by the Secretary of War on April 23, but with the 2nd Ohio still wearing the "Pennsylvania" clothing. However, on June 9 an unidentified member of the latter regiment wrote: "This morning part of our new uniforms were issued to us: the cap, pants, and shoes. The cap is of the famous lager beer style, blue trimmed with light blue cord and of the proportions of a good sized sugar loaf. The pants are of a coarse quality of cotton goods dyed blue in watercolors. It generally costs each man the sum of fifty cents to get a tailor to cut them down to the right size... ." The headgear described was almost certainly the high-crowned 1858-pattern forage cap, while the clothing was regular Federal issue.

The 14th through 23rd Ohio

The organization of the 11 remaining Ohio regiments progressed so slowly that the state reorganized them for three years' service. Meanwhile, in order to make use of the surplus companies accepted by the State Adjutant-General on April 26, a further ten infantry regiments numbered the 14th through 23rd Ohio were speedily raised for three months' service, and saw action in western Virginia. Of these, the 14th Ohio received 912 each of caps, cap covers, blouses, trousers, and flannel shirts by May 23. Their four-button sack coats were patterned after Federal issue, while shirts were gray and trousers probably sky-blue. When this regiment returned home after seeing action at Philippi, Laurel Hill, and Carrick's Ford, some of its men were reported in the *Columbus Gazette* of July 26 to be "dressed up in Secession suits."

Prior to its departure from Columbus on May 25, the 16th Ohio was "without uniforms, and in their [red] flannel shirts." A report in the *Cincinnati Daily Commercial* of May 28 stated that "This dress parade was by men not in their uniforms, but in their shirt sleeves. Scarcely an officer, either, was in uniform or had even a side arm." Although this regiment received 500 pairs of gray pants with black seam stripes on June 26 (see issuance of gray clothing, below), it was still lacking sufficient uniforms by the end of the month; four days later the *Daily Ohio Statesman* reported that 20 men had been arrested for insubordination, said to be "caused by dissatisfaction with their clothing." The regiment received "uniform Pants" on July 2. At least three companies, and possibly the whole unit, were finally issued Federal-pattern blue sack coats on July 24 – just a week before their tour of duty ended. As a result, Pvt Oscar Ladley of Co E wrote: "We would be laughed at if we had been sent home in our rags."

Sent to guard the Baltimore & Ohio Railroad in West Virginia, the 18th Ohio received 950 blouses plus gray pants, and 451 caps and cap covers, during June. When this regiment mustered-out it was reported in the *Daily Ohio Statesman* of August 10 to have "accepted without a murmur, the uniforms furnished them by the State authorities, and which were unfit to cover the wax statues of stationary museums."

Due to a shortage of blue-dyed wool cloth, the Columbus quartermasters had to contract for gray satinet to make 5,750 "round" jackets that were issued to the 15th, 17th, 19th, and 20th Ohio. Based on photographic evidence, these garments were fastened by either eight or nine buttons, with two small buttons on each cuff, and had plain standing collars and shoulder flaps. Matching trousers had black seam stripes. Caps were dark blue, and waist belts were fastened with oval "OVM" plates. When inspected by Adjutant-General Henry Carrington at Wheeling, VA, on June 10, the 15th Ohio was found to be wearing "worthless pantaloons." Three days later the *Cincinnati Daily Commercial* commented that the shoes the regiment claimed to be "paper-soled" were plundered from Confederate stores taken at Philippi.

Serving as an enlisted man in Co K, 17th Ohio, Alexis Cope recalled: "The uniforms issued to the men turned out to be shoddy, of the poorest kind, and were soon so ragged that trousers and… jackets, had to be patched and held

Identified as Ohio volunteers by their oval "OVM" belt plates, these men wear gray jackets and trousers with dark blue caps. Although both are armed with M1842 smoothbore muskets their accoutrements vary: the man on the left has the large, flat .58cal cartridge box suspended from his shoulder belt, while his comrade has the rather smaller, thicker .69cal box. (Library of Congress, Prints & Photographs Division, [LC-DIG-ppmsca-31659])

This heavily armed gray-clad volunteer of either the 15th, 17th, 19th, or 20th Ohio holds a musket, has a Colt revolver tucked into his belt, and poses with an M1832 Artillery sword resting across his lap. (Follett House Museum, Sandusky, Ohio)

together by pieces of the red flannel shirts… The men made a joke of trying to mend their worn out gray uniforms… and vied with each other in producing the most grotesque effects. On some… the patches were so many and so broad that in the general effect the red seemed to predominate."

INDIANA

Required to provide six regiments, Governor Oliver Morton of Indiana issued a call for "loyal and patriotic men," and within a week nearly three times the number of volunteers needed had gathered at Camp Morton, Indianapolis. The required regiments had been organized by April 27, being numbered 6th through 11th Indiana in deference to the five Indiana regiments that had been raised for the Mexican War (1846–48).

While volunteer militia – such as the City Greys and Independent Zouaves of Indianapolis – were suitably uniformed, many new units struggled to acquire a military appearance. According to Sgt Andrew Grayson, who enlisted in Co E, 6th Indiana on April 17, his company commander presented each man with "a black 'glazed' cap, to appear more in uniform, which pretty well cleaned out that style of cap in Madison." On April 22, the *Daily Sentinel* of Indianapolis reported that "many entire companies wore red shirts without coats, and black pants, making a uniform that in a pinch would do right well for immediate service."

Meanwhile, on April 25, the State Quartermaster-General T. Morris published proposals for "Coat and pants of strong, cheap woolen goods," and a "Felt Hat or Woolen Cap." Each volunteer would also receive two flannel shirts to be of "gray mixture, with pockets, cuffs and collars," and "High-quarter Shoes." A report in the *Daily Sentinel* dated May 2 indicated that Morris had awarded contracts for nine-button jackets with stand-up collars. The pants were made in a matching color with black stripes on the outer seams. The color of the cloth for both jacket and trousers varied considerably, from "sheep's gray" to a bluish "cadet" gray, to dark blue, to light blue "jean." The fabric used also varied according to circumstances and general availability. In addition to "jean cloth," early Indiana uniforms were cut from "cassinette," "satinette," or "cassimere."

By mid-May these six regiments began to receive uniforms. Sergeant Grayson of the 6th Indiana recorded that it was "an inferior article of gray, pants and roundabout, and big hat to suit, together with stoga [*sic*] shoes." On May 19, Pvt Valentine Thuma, 8th Indiana Infantry, wrote in his diary: "The suit consists of pants and roundabout. The clothes fit very imperfectly…"

Probably photographed at Indianapolis during May/June 1861, Pvt James T. Mathews, Putnam Union Guards (Co F, 10th Indiana Infantry) wears a light blue jeans uniform, as furnished under contract to the state by the outfitters G.W. Geissendorff at a cost of $6.50 per suit. Fastened at the front by nine US infantry "eagle" buttons, it has two smaller buttons on each cuff. His gray felt hat with red, white and blue hat cord was supplied by William Dodd & Co of Cincinnati, Ohio. (Anne S.K. Brown Military Collection)

On May 29, the *Indianapolis Daily Journal* reported that the 9th Indiana was wearing "a complete uniform of sheep's gray, durable and strong," when it departed for western Virginia. There is evidence that this regiment later received replacement uniforms; on July 16 a letter from Col James Steadman, 14th Ohio, published in the *Cincinnati Daily Commercial* stated: "I examined a jacket that a Georgia corporal left in his retreat... It is nearly like that of the 9th Indiana regiment: gray cloth with black velvet facings on the collar and cuffs."

On May 23, the Indianapolis *Daily Sentinel* praised the new uniforms issued to the 10th Indiana, stating: "The jacket and pants are made of a good article of blue jeans, and look much better to our notion than the gray and dove colored cassinet." The next day a reporter for the same newspaper saw this regiment parade, and was "struck with the neatness of their uniforms." Their blue jeans jacket and pants were described as well made and better fitting than any others he had noticed.

Concerning headgear for the 6th through 10th Indiana, on May 3 the *Daily Sentinel* reported: "The hat adopted for the five regiments... will be found to be a very comfortable covering for the head, and with its loop on the side will look neat. It will be far better for the men than caps, and will afford protection from the sun without adding much more weight than the cap." The exact color of these hats seems to have varied from light gray to light brown. As the 6th Indiana passed through Cincinnati on May 30, the *Daily Commercial* reported them as wearing "gray felt hats looped up with red cord." In his diary Pvt V. Thuma, 8th Indiana Infantry, wrote on May 24: "We received our hats today. They are gray, rough and ready with the left side buttoned up." The 9th Indiana was later reported to be wearing "gray slouch hats with red and black tassels." In the case of the 10th Indiana, a newspaper account of the regiment's color presentation ceremony on May 29, 1861 simply remarked that its men wore "gray felt hats."

A "smoky ribbon" of zouaves

The 11th Indiana was organized at Indianapolis on April 25 under the command of Col Lewis Wallace (who would later become famous as the author of *Ben-Hur*). The next day the *Daily Sentinel* reported: "Colonel Wallace informs us that the regiment will be uniformed as Zouaves... but the color will be gray. As the government does not send out such [a] uniform, it is probable that they will be made to order." The uniform acquired by Wallace's Zouaves was purchased from Eli Hall, merchant tailor of Indianapolis. In his autobiography published in 1906, Wallace wrote that "There was nothing of the flashy, Algerian colors in the uniform of the Eleventh Indiana; no fez, a headgear exclusively Mohammedan, and therefore to be religiously avoided by Christians; no red breeches, no red or yellow sash with tassels big as early cabbages. Our outfit was of the tamest gray twilled goods, not unlike home-made jeans – a visor cap, French pattern, its top of red cloth not larger than the palm of one's hand; blue flannel shirt with open neck; a jacket Greekish in form, edged with narrow binding, the red scarcely noticeable; breeches baggy, but not petticoated; button gaiters connecting below the knees with the breeches, and strapped over the shoe. The effect was to magnify the men, though in line two thousand yards off they looked like a smoky ribbon long-drawn out."

This enlisted man of the 11th Indiana, also known as Wallace's Zouaves, wears the uniform purchased for his regiment by its commander, Col Lew Wallace. Described as being of "the tamest gray twilled goods," the jacket was trimmed with red, and the gray chasseur-pattern cap had a red top. (Daniel Miller Collection)

Wearing an example of the gray uniform acquired by Illinois during late April/early May 1861, this unidentified volunteer, possibly of the 7th Illinois, wears a five-button jacket with standing collar and epaulet straps. His pants are also gray, while his cap appears to be dark blue. He holds a Model 1816 musket converted to percussion. (Allen Cebula Collection)

This unidentified member of the 12th Illinois Volunteers, also known as "The First Scotch Regiment," wears a sky-blue Federal overcoat and an example of the regiment's tam-o'-shanter-style cap with a shallow plaid band (see Plate C4). The 12th Illinois' Col John McArthur had previously commanded the Highland Guard, a Scottish volunteer militia company organized in Chicago in 1856. (Library of Congress, Prints & Photographs Division, [LC-DIG-ppmsca-36917])

ILLINOIS

The Cairo Expedition

About 40 companies volunteered within 24 hours following the executive call for six regiments from Illinois. In acknowledgment of the six units which had served in the Mexican War, Illinois too numbered her new regiments in sequence with them, from the 7th Illinois upward. Before these regiments could be organized, however, a provisional militia force took the field. On April 19, Secretary of War Cameron telegraphed Governor Richard Yates instructing him to send troops as a matter of urgency to Cairo, the southernmost city in Illinois. A strategic point where the Mississippi and Ohio rivers meet, Cairo was considered of great importance in Union plans to use the Mississippi River route to invade the South.

Two days later, BrigGen Richard Swift, commanding the 2nd Brigade, Sixth Division, Illinois Militia, left Chicago with the "Cairo Expedition" composed of six volunteer militia companies. These were the Chicago Light Artillery; Companies A and B of a Zouave regiment being formed in that city; the Union Cadets, composed of German immigrants; the Lincoln Rifles, and the Hardin Infantry. These troops were followed the next day by three artillery companies plus an additional infantry company, all from counties near Chicago. By May 20 about 5,000 troops were stationed at Camp Defiance, Cairo, but a letter to the *Boston Evening Transcript* stated that "A majority of them have no uniforms, and are dressed just as they came from the fields and stores."

On the same day that these troops left for Cairo, a "Military Finance Committee" was formed in Chicago in order to provide this force with uniforms. A report in the *Chicago Daily Times* dated April 22 confirms that the Committee placed an order with an unknown New York company amounting to $6,400, for "500 uniforms of coats and pants, and 200 Zouave caps, to be distributed thus: 200 suits to companies 'A' and 'B' Zouaves; 150 suits to Capt [James] Smith's company [Chicago Light Artillery]; 100 to Capt [Fred] Harding's [*sic*] company; and the remainder to some of the other Chicago companies at Springfield or Chicago." However, none of the clothing ordered by this Committee had been received by May 16. As a result, the Chicago volunteers were "almost destitute of clothing, their citizen's dress having worn out in the hardships they have endured at Cairo and vicinity." Hence, a new order was placed with clothiers A.D. Titsworth & Co. of Chicago for 1,000 uniforms to consist of "the army fatigue dress in 'cadet gray' cloth, a full suit, with long surtout [overcoat] and heavy cape." The Committee also purchased "1,100 gray woolen shirts."

Chicago and New York procurement

Elsewhere, local efforts were underway to clothe additional Chicago volunteers. By the end of the month a "Sewing Hall" had been established in McVicker's Theater Building, and by May 21 the ladies had produced "hundreds of under-shirts, uniform shirts and pants, [and] caps."

As volunteers gathered at Springfield, IL, the state authorities also attempted to provide uniforms. It was initially hoped that Illinois volunteers would be clothed by the Federal government. On April 23, the *Illinois Daily State Register* published a set of orders regarding the organization of this force, which stated: "Only such clothing as is absolutely necessary will be allowed." The state would subsequently regret this action, as recruits began to arrive with nothing but the clothes they stood up in. Letters of complaint soon appeared in the local newspapers. Private Marrion Morrison, Co D, 9th Illinois, wrote: "Many of the soldiers supposed that they would be supplied with clothing by the government so took little with them… many had no change of clothing for three months. Some of the companies were clothed with such a uniform as they had supplied themselves." On May 28, in a letter to the *Chicago Evening Journal*, an unknown volunteer with the 12th Illinois at Camp Bissell, near Caseyville, wrote: "But few of the companies are uniformed, and those have been at the expense of the various cities from which they came."

Meanwhile, on April 29, the *Chicago Daily Tribune* reported: "There have been received in this city by United States Express Company, destined for Springfield… thirteen packages of 500 pounds each containing uniforms made by a New York firm for our Illinois troops." On May 14, the same newspaper stated that a Chicago clothing firm (probably A.D. Titsworth, & Co.) had "contracted to manufacture and deliver in Springfield four thousand uniforms… the suits to be gray, after the pattern of those worn by the Seventh New York Regiment." Photographic evidence indicates that some Illinois volunteers eventually received short plain gray coats with standing collars fastened with seven buttons, matching gray pants, and gray caps. As the 12th Illinois, or "The First Scotch Regiment," was formed by John McArthur, former commander of a Scottish militia company in Chicago, its choice of headgear was distinctive: a rough approximation of a tam-o'-shanter, with a plaid headband.

This enlisted man of the Johnson Guard (Co I, 4th New Jersey Foot Militia) wears a dark frock coat with light trim around the collar and cuffs and down the front. Another enlisted man from this unit was photographed wearing exactly the same type of checkered trousers, which perhaps indicates that they were part of this company's uniform. (Author's collection)

Headgear

Following criticism of both "the color and style" of red zouave caps worn by the zouave volunteer companies of Chicago – which offered "too good a mark for the enemy," covered "only the top of the head," and failed to give "shelter from sun, and inclement weather" – a recommendation was made in the local press that felt hats were more suitable. On May 1 a report in the *Chicago Daily Times* advised that "There never was manufactured for rough use a better head covering than the soft felt hat and its adoption by the army was a sensible one. It may be slouched to protect the face and neck, is susceptible of a large variety of shapes and modifications, none of which, however, should interfere with a moderate breadth of brim."

On May 24, and as a possible response, Chicago hatters J. & A. Herzog advertised in the same journal that they were "manufacturing the new style Havelock Cap." During this same period James M. Loomis, another hatter in the city, invented a "new style of forage cap" which he had made in New York City; this was described as "resembling an ordinary felt hat, the rim dishing deeply, turned downwards behind and cut away from side to side in front where a neat leather visor is substituted. Thus the neck and head

are well protected, leaving the front clear and unobstructed." (This style of cap predated the headgear patented by Jonathan F. Whipple, and produced by his Seamless Clothing Manufacturing Company of New York City during the summer of 1861.) The *Chicago Daily Tribune* concluded its report on the latter development in Chicago on June 3 by stating that "Mr. Loomis has already received large orders from our State troops at Cairo. They will be sure to take wherever introduced, as very nearly combining the… utilities of cap and Havelock."

Although Loomis supplied "Havelock hats" to several three-month regiments, they proved unpopular with the troops. Writing home on August 29, Pvt James M. Swales, Co A, 10th Illinois, called the headgear "ugly as the devil." On October 11, Pvt George D. Carrington, Co B, 11th Illinois, agreed: "Drew new hats. We don't like them." Thirteen days later he added: "We bought red caps to wear."

NEW JERSEY

In response to the request to supply four regiments, Governor Charles Olden of New Jersey ordered each of his four militia divisions to furnish one regiment. Within 15 days a sufficient number of companies had volunteered to complete the quota. Designated "Foot Militia," the four regiments of the 1st New Jersey Brigade left the state for Washington, DC, on May 4.

Although there is no evidence that New Jersey had issued state dress regulations for its troops during the 1850s, the Hudson Brigade, Second Division, adopted a uniform in 1858 which consisted of "mazarine blue pants, dark blue frock coat, cap of pattern of 71st [New York Militia] regiment." In 1859 the Newark Brigade, Second Division, also adopted "dark blue frock coats and light blue trousers with white stripe." Infantry were distinguished by white belts and riflemen by black belts. Despite this growing conformity, the uniforms of the New Jersey militia were considered inadequate for field service in 1861. The *Atlantic Democrat* of May 4 summed up the situation during the first few weeks of war: "There is no uniformity, as some regiments are equipped at home better than those that depend on the State. This is not right, but the exigency of the case, perhaps justifies the difference."

In response, the Federal government uniformed the 1st New Jersey Foot Militia, which left – according to the *Daily State Gazette*, of Trenton, dated May 1 – "having also overcoats and blankets." Meanwhile, Governor Olden appointed a Board of Commissioners to provide a uniform, and the citizens of New Jersey set about

ABOVE This unidentified New Jersey enlisted man shows light-colored trim around the bottom of the collar, on the cuffs and non-regulation epaulet or "bridle" straps. His light blue trousers have a narrow seam stripe or welt. (Author's collection)

clothing some of their volunteers. Organized at Trenton, the 2nd New Jersey was in receipt of clothing and equipment before the end of April costing $23,000, and paid for entirely by private subscription by the citizens of Jersey City. Following his visit to Camp Olden in South Trenton on April 28, a correspondent of the *Daily State Gazette* wrote: "At the Quarter Master's tent… great activity prevailed… and the constant demand for coats, over-coats, pants, shoes, [and] knapsacks, showed that 'service' was at least expected."

According to the same newspaper, the 3rd and 4th regiments received clothing paid for by State Quartermaster-General Lewis Perrine. That received by the Olden Guards (Co A), Wilkinson Guards (Co C), and Jersey Blues (Co D), 3rd Regiment, plus the Anderson Guards (Co H, 4th Regt) was made by the "Ladies of Trenton." First formed in Camden during January, the Stevens' Zouaves were still wearing their zouave uniforms, possibly based on those of the Chicago Zouave Cadets, when they enlisted as Co G, 4th New Jersey.

By May 18, the Board of Commission appointed to choose a "Regulation Uniform" for the New Jersey Militia had chosen a "Blue Coat, Light Blue Pants and Army Cockade Hat." It is not known whether this was a retrospective description of the uniform provided before the four regiments left for Washington, DC, or replaced the clothing supplied before their departure. What is certain is that, according to the State Quartermaster-General's report, the Newark-based firm of N. Perry & Co supplied uniforms at a total cost of $30,216; another 29 firms also provided uniforms.

While at Camp Scott near Washington, DC, the New Jersey volunteers were issued on June 12 with straw hats and linen pants which seemed more appropriate for the hotter climate in Virginia. According to the *Daily State Gazette*, "The variety of shapes into which a straw hat can be converted, was never before demonstrated. Three cornered hats, and cocked hats, and hats all brim, and hats with the brim all gone to the crown… are to be seen through the camp."

MASSACHUSETTS

The Commonwealth of Massachusetts provided five regiments of infantry, one rifle battalion, and one light artillery battery. The militia system of that state consisted of a series of undersized regiments, plus a myriad of independent battalions and companies, most of which wore distinctive uniforms in defiance of the state regulations issued in the 1850s. Hence, when the call for troops was issued and the state was requested to provide 20 companies of infantry, the regiments with the most complete organization – the 3rd, 4th, 6th, and 8th Massachusetts Volunteer Militia (MVM) – were ordered out. After assembly at Boston, the 6th followed by the 8th were dispatched to Washington, DC, while the other two were sent to Fortress Monroe on the Virginia Peninsula.

Many of the volunteers making up these regiments were variously attired in prewar uniforms mixed with civilian clothing, some of the latter being hastily given a military appearance. Arriving at North Easton for service with the Easton Light Infantry, Robert Dollard recalled: "It was the work of a few minutes to… have our white stripes, about an inch wide, sewed down the outer seams of our black doeskin Sunday trousers, and slip them on with our blue uniform dress coats, ornamented

William H. Cook of the Cushing Guards (Co A, 8th Massachusetts Volunteer Militia) wears a pale, five-button fatigue shirt with narrow trim around the pockets and front placket. Note two unexplained buttons high above the pockets, matching pants, and darker cap. (Michael J. McAfee Collection)

OPPOSITE First Sgt Ellis Hamilton of Co G, 4th New Jersey (Stevens' Zouaves). He became a lieutenant in the 15th New Jersey at the age of 16, and rose to the rank of captain before, aged just 18, he was killed in action in the Wilderness in 1864. (Special Collections and University Archives, Rutgers University Archives)

Sergeant Charles S. Emmerton wears the uniform in which the Salem Light Infantry (also known as the Salem Zouaves) – Co I, 8th MVM – arrived in Washington, DC, on May 8, 1861. His dark blue jacket is trimmed across the chest with scarlet braid, and his cap is red with a blue band plus yellow trim. (USAMHI)

with white epaulets… and adjust our hats, as tall as the ordinary stovepipe article."

The state provided each man with additional items of clothing and equipage in preparation for the forthcoming campaign. According to the *Boston Herald* of April 17, the 6th MVM was furnished with "two blue flannel shirts, one pair of socks, and one pair of drawers." The 4th and 8th MVM received "overcoats," plus "one pair of boots and a Guernsey frock." The latter was described by Robert Dollard as "a gray woolen shirt" worn outside the trousers as "a frock coat, similar to General Burnside's [Rhode Island] regiment in the early part of the war, and… equipments were put on over this shirt."

For overcoats, the state purchased 6,000 yards of iron-gray beaver cloth during February in anticipation of "the inevitable conflict," which it had made up based on a pattern obtained after consultation with the US Army Quartermaster Department. The *Boston Herald* reported that the new coats for the volunteers were "speedily fitted to their backs" under the supervision of Maj George Clark, Jr, of the 2nd Brigade Staff. The report continued: "The coats are made of dark gray cloth, and look very neat and serviceable. They are of the army pattern, and comprise three sizes only – 'large,' 'small,' and 'middling.'" With stocks running low, the state contracted with Whitten, Hopkins & Co of Boston to supply 1,500 more overcoats, of which 1,000 were to be completed by April 23.

The poor quality of some clothing, and particularly the trousers, became apparent following the departure of Massachusetts troops for the front. According to the memoirs of Capt Luther Stephenson, commanding the Lincoln Light Infantry (Co I, 4th MVM), clothing was "poorly fitted to sustain the rough usage… and the results were oftentime ludicrous and amusing." At regular Sunday inspection, he continued, some of the men appeared in "overcoats, although the weather was warm and bright. This was to conceal their tattered clothing, and, in some instances, the fact that they had no trousers, and only their drawers to hide their nakedness. The contrast in appearance between our militia, with their torn, worn-out uniforms, and the companies of regulars who still remained in the fort [Monroe], was very marked and striking."

With an increase in the Federal call on April 16, Governor John Andrew ordered out the 5th MVM supplemented by companies from the 1st and 7th MVM, plus the 3rd Battalion and Boston Light Artillery, all of which left for Washington, DC, on April 21. With stocks of state overcoats depleted, these units received some Federal-issue overcoats, which the *Boston Herald* of April 28 described as being of "the infantry pattern, blue in color, and… heavier and of better quality than the State coats." State overcoats were furnished to the remaining volunteers even as they were "on their march to the [railroad] cars," the tailors at Whitten, Hopkins & Co having worked day and night to produce them.

By April 24, the "Committee of the City Council on Military Supplies" in Boston had chosen a more suitable uniform for the volunteers from that city, having appropriated $100,000 for the purpose. After examining several patterns, they chose a semi-chasseur uniform, described in the *Boston Herald* thus: "… a sort of Garibaldi suit, made of heavy gray doeskin, and trimmed with red cord. The jacket is to be long bodied and short tailed, with regular military collar, and well lined throughout. The cap is of gray turned up with red, and the whole thing is neat and serviceable. Its cost is but about ten dollars." The Boston firm of George W. Simmons & Co was contracted to produce 1,000 of these uniforms. According to a report in the *Boston Daily Advertiser* of May 5, a large number of hands were employed "day and night" making "Coats and Pantaloons for the Troops" with "a liberal price paid for the work." Once completed, the clothing was delivered to the Military Equipment Depot, and was issued to about 16 companies of volunteers enlisted in the city.

In order to outfit volunteers elsewhere in the state, State Quartermaster-General John Reed contracted on May 8 with Haughton, Sawyer, & Co of Boston to supply "3000 suits of light wool uniforms, of a gray color," which were based on the pattern produced for the Boston troops. A major supplier of "Army Equipments," this firm also had stores at Astor House, New York; Continental House, in Philadelphia; Briggs House, in Chicago; and Neil House, at Columbus, Ohio. By September it had "extensive contracts with the US government and from eight or ten of the Northern and Western states" – and, according to a report in the *Boston Daily Advertiser* of September 13, the firm was also suspected of being "engaged in the business of furnishing army equipments and materials for the use of the rebels."

The Edmands hat

Haughton, Sawyer, & Co additionally supplied a distinctive form of headgear for Massachusetts troops, which was also received by some Ohio three-year regiments, including the 34th Ohio (also known as the Piatt Zouaves). On May 2, the *Salem Register* reported that "a style of head dress... combining several suggestions of practical men who have seen service in warm latitudes, has been prepared and offered to our State authorities by General B.[enjamin] F. Edmands. It is in appearance a combination of the old continental, the army and the Kossuth hats, and is designed to afford the best means of protecting the head from the sun's rays and consequently sunstroke." Designed by Gen Edmands, a member of the Boston Committee, this hat was made of gray felt and buttoned up on all four sides, its front being embellished with a vertical strip of red trim. Photographic evidence indicates that the 3rd, 4th, and 6th MVM were issued with this headgear.

As so often, much of the state clothing issued did not match up to expectations. In a letter dated July 13, a correspondent of the Lowell *Daily Citizen & News* wrote of the 6th MVM that "The uniform of the regiment is nearly worn out, and looks rather seedy, but it will be worn home to show our people how shabbily the three months' volunteers have been treated by the state of Massachusetts." Upon this regiment's return to Lowell their poorly-made uniforms were described by the same journal as "suits of Garibaldi gray," which made them look more like "rebel zouaves" than "the good Union soldiers they were."

During his visit to the "Photograph and Ambrotype Gallery" of Benson C. Hazelton on Washington Street, Boston, this unidentified volunteer of the 4th MVM wears an "Edmands"-pattern hat, and a state-issue gray single-breasted infantry overcoat. (Author's collection)

Aged 23, Enoch Westcott was living in Westbrook, Maine, when he enlisted as a corporal in the 2nd Company of the Portland Rifle Guards (mustered-in as Co I, 1st Maine Volunteers). After nearly three months' service at the Federal capital he was taken ill with typhoid fever on July 29. Carried in the "sick car" when his unit returned home on August 3, he died nine days later, being the only man that the regiment lost during its service. In this *carte de visite* copy of an original cased image he wears the seven-button gray frock coat with tall standing collar that was hastily supplied to the 1st Maine by a Boston merchant tailor. (Author's collection)

MAINE

Following the outbreak of Civil War the legislature of Maine met in extra session, and authorized the raising of ten regiments to serve a two-year term of enlistment by what became known as the "Ten Regiment Bill." However, in response to Lincoln's call for one three-month regiment, the first of these units was mustered into Federal service for the shorter period only. Recruitment for the 1st Maine Volunteers began within the First Division, Volunteer Militia on April 20, and in a week its ten companies were full and encamped around Portland. A total of 779 volunteers were mustered into this regiment on May 3. The 1st Maine was eventually ordered to Washington, DC, on June 1, where it remained until August 1. Spending its entire service in the defenses of the capital, it saw no combat, and was mustered-out on August 5.

Much of the clothing for the enlisted men was acquired in Boston, Massachusetts. Enlisting in the Portland Light Guards (Co C, 1st Maine) on May 3, John Gould recorded in the regimental history: "We had our uniforms and clothing issued to us as fast as they could be made up or bought." His diary entry dated April 28 stated: "We were marched to the new City Hall, where we each received a pair of woollen shirts, two pairs of woollen drawers, two pairs woollen stockings, and one pair of shoes with leather strings, the shoes being the great, wide kind you see in shops on the wharves, where fishermen trade."

On April 30 a letter published in the *Lewiston Daily Evening Journal* stated that "Yesterday and to-day have been spent in the armory, and being marched down, in squads, to the Clothing rooms, to be fitted out with clothes and shoes." Of this occasion John Gould wrote: "We received our overcoats, pantaloons, haversacks and knapsacks… The overcoat is gray with the Massachusetts brass button… and is not a bad coat; the pantaloons are of poorer stuff and made in a hurry; color a mixture of gray, red and brown." On May 9 he wrote that "Our company had their under coats and rubber blankets distributed… The coats are made of a very poor gray cloth and have the Maine buttons; the overcoats are being altered, receiving the Maine button." According to photographic evidence, the frock coats supplied to the 1st Maine were plain gray, with a tall standing collar and a seven-button front. Color and trim on 1858-pattern caps appeared to vary between companies. Shirts were gray, and might be either pull-over or button-front.

The inadequacies of Boston procurement

The clothing issued to the 1st Maine proved unsatisfactory. The poorly-made pantaloons were cause for concern as soon as the regiment reached the heat of the Federal capital in early June. Gould recalled: "The first thing we did after arriving at our quarters was to strip… down to shirt and drawers… ripping out the trowsers lining." Regarding their heavy gray frock coats, he observed: "We had our usual drills by company and regiment, and dress parades every evening all in our shirt sleeves, which was the only comfortable rig we had." On May 27, the Lewiston *Daily Evening Journal* reported: "We understand that the 'committee on military expenditure'… have demanded, and obtained such a reduction on the bill for clothing purchased in Boston for the 1st Regiment, as to make the whole purchase of a character (as regards price) that they should satisfy all complaints from every quarter."

On June 4, the Washington *Evening Star* reported that the men of the regiment "complain with reason at the outrageous swindle perpetrated upon them by the Boston dealers who supplied their uniforms, the cloth and the workmanship being so inferior that the clothes are already falling to pieces." In a letter to the Bangor *Whig and Courier*, dated July 8, a member of the 2nd Maine commented on the condition of the 1st Regiment: their clothing was in "such a state that they could not be moved properly" as "fifty or sixty [men] had no shoes to their feet."

On receipt of pay on July 11, many Maine men bought "sutler-stuff" to replace their unsatisfactory state uniforms. Gould commented that the Lewiston Zouaves (Co K) acquired "blue flannel coats and white gaiters." At the end of their period of service members of this regiment made an effigy representing a 1st Maine soldier as a mark of their "contempt for the uniform," and, placing it on a pole, "tried to burn it, but it 'stood fire' well."

Found in a trunk with other militia items in Keene, NH, this image shows an unidentified volunteer a few days after his enlistment in April 1861. Many men were gifted revolvers by fundraising groups, and this man is holding what seems to be a .22cal Smith & Wesson pocket model. (Author's collection)

NEW HAMPSHIRE

The Granite State was asked to provide a single regiment. Although a thriving militia existed in New Hampshire, Governor Ichabod Goodwin did not feel he had the right to require them to serve. Instead, recruiting offices were opened throughout the state and new volunteers were recruited (although one Volunteer Militia company, the Abbott Guards of Manchester, did enlist in its entirety). The new companies rendezvoused at Concord, and the organization of the regiment progressed rapidly.

These unidentified privates wear the gray dress uniform provided for the 1st New Hampshire by the State Quartermaster-General in May 1861. The man at left is clearly seated so as to show off his "spike-tail" coat to best advantage; the high standing collars and closed cuffs were trimmed with narrow red cord. The trousers were plain gray, but the chasseur-pattern caps had a red band. (Author's collection)

Joseph Abbott, the State Adjutant-General, put out contracts for uniforms and equipment. On April 26, the *New Hampshire Sentinel* advised that this would consist of a "Cadet gray coat and pants, gray overcoat, gray fatigue cap, two flannel shirts [and] one pair of shoes." According to the "Minutes of the New Hampshire legislature" published in the *Patriot & State Gazette* on July 3, the coat, pants, and overcoats for the 1st New Hampshire were made by Whiting, Galloupe, Bliss & Co and Whitten, Hopkins & Co of Boston, at a cost of $7 for the coat and pants combined, and $7.87 for the overcoats. The regiment began to receive its uniforms on May 17, on which date an unidentified volunteer wrote in the Amherst *Farmer's Cabinet*: "We got our uniforms today. The cut of the coat is 'swallow-tail.' Caps, small, gray, military, with a red stripe around them." Unusual and old-fashioned, the dress coats worn by the New Hampshire men had plain tails without turnbacks or pocket flaps, but were trimmed around the high standing collar and the cuffs with narrow red cord, and had a single row of six (or in some cases nine) yellow metal buttons bearing the state coat of arms.

The rest of the uniform worn by the 1st New Hampshire was made locally as well as in Boston. The gray chasseur-pattern caps with red bands were supplied by George A. Barnes, a merchant based at Manchester, NH, and by Klouse & Co of Boston. Although photographic evidence indicates that many men wore buttons on their cap fronts bearing the state coat of arms, a drunken man accused of being "a scallawag in the regiment" was stripped of his uniform, including "the letters on his cap," on June 14, according to a report in the *New Hampshire Statesman*.

Service dress

Aware that his regiment was in need of a service dress, Col Mason Tappan inserted an appeal in the *New Hampshire Statesman* dated May 18 requesting "one thousand flannel blouses" to supplement "the thick uniforms" with which the regiment was provided. It is unclear whether the State or Federal government responded, but the 1st New Hampshire was indeed issued with blue flannel fatigue blouses. On arrival in Washington, DC, to join the ranks of Co F in late May, Thomas Livermore received a uniform consisting of "a blue blouse, gray trousers, and gray cap with a red band."

Assigned to Gen Robert Patterson's Army of the Shenandoah, the 1st New Hampshire took part in the action at Conrad's Ferry in June, and, after a march to Maryland and then back to Virginia, returned home. By the time it mustered-out on August 9 its uniforms and shoes were worn out. Recalling its period of encampment at Martinsburg, VA, on July 8–15, regimental historian Stephen Abbott wrote: "The clothes of the men, which were poor at best, had become much worn, and they were almost shoeless… Many were the shifts to which they resorted to cover their nakedness. In one case three of the boys found a strip of cloth on which was painted: 'Pies and Cakes,'" which was converted into three patches for their pantaloons. Another made a similar use of the discarded covering of a ham, and appeared on dress parade labeled: "Sugar-Cured Hams for Family Use."

(continued on page 33)

PENNSYLVANIA
1: Private, Sarsfield Rifles, 21st Pennsylvania Infantry
2: Musician, Philadelphia Zouave Corps, 1st Pennsylvania Inf
3: Private, 2nd Pennsylvania Inf (redesignated 19th Pennsylvania)

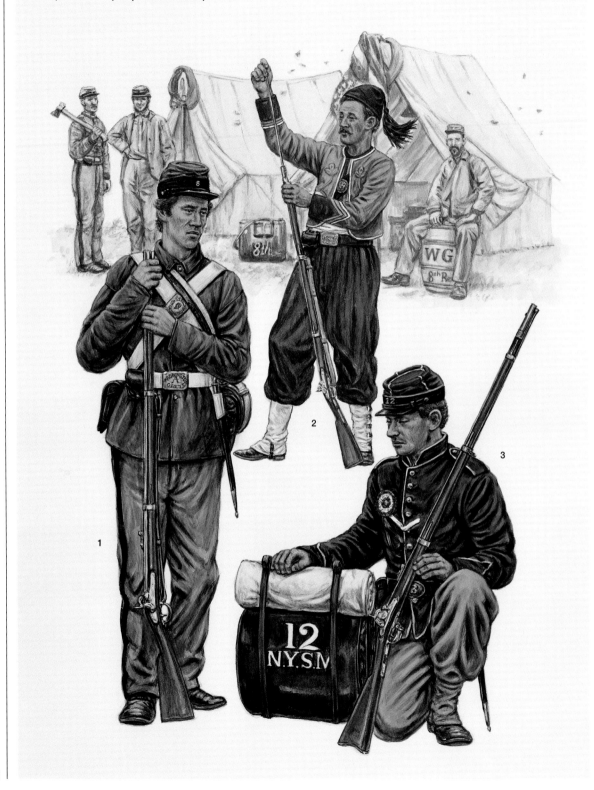

B

OHIO, INDIANA, & ILLINOIS
1: NCO, 19th Ohio Volunteer Infantry
2: Private, Co K, 16th Ohio (Springfield Greys)
3: Private, 9th Indiana Infantry
4: Private, 12th Illinois Volunteers (The First Scotch Regiment)

MAINE, NEW HAMPSHIRE, & DISTRICT OF COLUMBIA
1: Private, 1st Maine Volunteer Militia
2: Private, 1st New Hampshire Volunteers, full dress
3: Private, 1st New Hampshire Volunteers, fatigue dress
4: Pvt, Co E, 4th Bn, District of Columbia Militia (Washington Zouaves)

RHODE ISLAND & CONNECTICUT
1: Officer, 1st Rhode Island Detached Militia
2: Kady Brownell, attached 1st Rhode Island Detached Militia
3: Private, 1st Connecticut Volunteers
4: Private, Co A, 1st Connecticut Volunteers

F

MICHIGAN, WISCONSIN, & VERMONT

1: Private, 1st Michigan Volunteers
2: Cpl, Co A, 1st Wisconsin Volunteers (Milwaukee Light Guard)
3: Private, 1st Vermont Volunteers

DELAWARE, MINNESOTA, & IOWA
1: Private, 1st Delaware Volunteer Militia
2: Private, 1st Minnesota Volunteers
3: Pvt, Co G, 1st Iowa Infantry (German Rifles)

H

VERMONT

The Green Mountain State was assigned a quota of one regiment. Accordingly, Governor Erastus Fairbanks issued orders to mobilize the Active Militia, and an emergency session of the legislature met on April 25. In order to raise this regiment the ten uniformed militia companies with the fullest ranks were ordered to rendezvous at Rutland. An 1836 graduate of the US Military Academy who had served for 23 years with the US Army, John Phelps of Brattleboro was chosen to command the 1st Vermont, also known as the "Green Mountain Boys." As each of its companies possessed prewar uniforms of various colors, a regimental uniform was required for the 1st Vermont, and this was acquired in Boston by State Quartermaster-General George Davis, who, according to the *Vermont Phoenix* of Brattleboro dated April 25, also obtained "overcoats, blankets and general camp equipment."

In the meantime, the state proposed to supply each volunteer with "1 coat, 1 fatigue cap, 2 pairs woollen socks, 1 knapsack, 1 trowsers, 2 flannel shirts, 1 pair shoes, 1 haversack, 1 overcoat, 2 flannel drawers, 1 blanket, 1 canteen." Four days later, the *St Albans Messenger* was able to report that "Their uniforms are being made with all possible haste, and will undoubtedly be ready by the time marching orders are received."

Mustered into US service on May 8, the 1st Vermont arrived at Fortress Monroe, VA, five days later. While passing through Troy, New York, the Vermonters were described in the *Messenger* of May 8 as being dressed in "serviceably gray uniforms with glittering muskets and tightly strapped knapsacks." A New York City reporter commented that they did not attract attention, because "a sober gray does not dazzle the eyes." On May 14, the Windsor *Vermont Chronicle* added that "All hands wear the Green Mountain sprig [in their caps]." Numbering 779 men, the 1st Vermont was considered by Gen Benjamin Butler to be one of the best regiments under his command. Occupying Hampton on May 23, it was the first regiment in the service of the US to take possession of Virginia soil.

However, the gray clothing of the 1st Vermont quickly deteriorated on campaign. An officer wrote on May 18 that the men were suffering from the "wearing out of their uniforms, particularly the pantaloons." Despite these shortcomings, all the regiment appears to have received during the remainder of its service was havelocks by May 23, and more shoes by June 13.[3] Having sustained two killed and three wounded when five of its companies took part in the engagement at Big Bethel on June 10, the 1st Vermont returned home on August 5.

This volunteer may have belonged to the New England Guards (Co F, 1st Vermont), enlisted at Northfield. He wears a fine checked shirt and gray military trousers with inch-wide seam stripes. It is unclear whether he is wearing a shop apron or a medical sling, the latter indicating that he may have been wounded. The young girl standing by his side has short-cropped hair; this suggests that she has just recovered from an illness, since the cutting of hair was believed to reduce a fever. (Marius Peladeau Collection)

Discovered at Dummerston, VT, this tintype shows three members of the Green Mountain Guards, a militia company from Swanton in the northwestern part of the state. Before enlistment as Co A, 1st Vermont Volunteers this unit wore dark green trousers and slightly lighter green seven-button coats. They hold M1855 rifle-muskets, which may have been part of the issue to the newly forming regiment. (Marius Peladeau Collection)

3   The classic "havelock" was a light cap cover with a falling neck curtain to protect against the sun, named after the British general of that name. See MAA 268, *British Troops in the Indian Mutiny, 1857–59*.

RHODE ISLAND

Governor William Sprague had already offered Lincoln "a force for the protection of the capital" when asked for one regiment of 37 officers and 743 men, so contingency plans were in place in Rhode Island. Within two days Sprague was able to report to Secretary of War Simon Cameron that the regiment was organized on the original basis, adding "We are using every exertion to be first in the field." Upon arrival at Providence, Ambrose Burnside, the former commander of the State Militia but then resident in New York, accepted command of the regiment. On April 18, the governor telegraphed Cameron that "Our troops are leaving in detachments today."

As Rhode Island lacked a full militia regiment prior to the Civil War, the ten companies that formed the 1st Regiment, Detached Militia were drawn from various existing companies of volunteer, or active, militia. This included such colorful units as the First Light Infantry, Pawtucket Light Guard, and Newport Artillery. Also lacking militia uniform regulations in 1861, the state needed a service dress for the regiment, and the responsibility for this task fell on Col Burnside. He chose a pull-over "hunting-shirt" – a blouse with falling collar and placket front opening, which was double-breasted for field and staff officers and single-breasted for company officers and enlisted men. Closed by three small brass state buttons, it also had a breast pocket fastened by a single button of the same type. The sleeves, cut full and gathered at the cuff, also fastened by a single button.

To produce this garment, 4,223 yards of blue flannel was purchased on April 16 at a cost of $2,006.46. Cloth sufficient to produce 1,000 blouses for the 1st Rhode Island was rushed to the store of H.A. Prescott in Providence, and the local ladies were advised that "The work must be done by to-night." According to a report published in the *Providence Daily Post* of April 20, work on blouses to be worn by the regiment was undertaken by the womenfolk of the local church congregations.

Procured from the Providence "hat manufactory" of Bowen & Pabodie, full-dress headgear for enlisted men consisted of a black felt hat which resembled the pattern-1858 US Army hat, but had a taller crown and a curled brim. Referred to as a "Kossuth hat," its brim was pinned up on the left side with a brass eagle insignia, and silver company letters were pinned to the front of the crown. Dress hats for officers were made of fur felt, with the brim pinned up with either the brass eagle or a cockade, and often sported black feather plumes. For fatigue wear, enlisted men wore blue chasseur-pattern forage caps with a metal company letter attached at the front. Officers wore what later became known as the "McDowell-style" cap, with tall crown and 1858-pattern "looped" horn insignia at the front.

Issue of the first batch of uniforms on April 19 was described by the *Providence Daily Post* as follows: "A busy scene was enacting at Mr. Prescott's store... throughout the day. It was there that the uniforms and clothing were given out, and detachments from each company were marched over there, when to each man was delivered the blue outside shirt, gray pants... and under-garments. They were then marched to Bowen & Pabodie's... when each obtained a black felt hat."

Moses B. Jenkins wears the dress hat, blue hunting-shirt, and gray pants issued to the 1st Rhode Island Detached Militia. A wealthy resident and landowner of Providence, RI, he enlisted in the Mechanic Rifles No. 2 on April 17, 1861. According to a report in the *New York Tribune*, he destroyed his ticket for "a passage to Europe that he might remain to fight in defence of the flag of his country." Under magnification his white cotton haversack can be seen to be stenciled "MB JENKINS/RI REGT." Compare this image with the reconstruction of the officer, Plate F1. (Michael J. McAfee Collection)

Instead of providing the regiment with overcoats, the state purchased 553 scarlet blankets with "black bar near the edge," at a cost of $5.50 per blanket. Rolled and carried diagonally on the soldier's back suspended from a leather strap, these blankets were slit at the center by order of Burnside so that they could be worn as a poncho. Of the wearing of this item, a correspondent of the New York *Evening Post* wrote on May 11 that each man had "a light scarlet blanket, which they wear with inimitable grace, pinning it in the shape of a coat, with a skill unobtainable to ordinary mortals."

When the regiment returned home at the end of its three-month period of service on July 25, 1861, the well-worn "war suits" of the 1st Rhode Island were reported by the *Providence Daily Journal* as consisting of "tattered tunics, dilapidated hats, more than one garnished with bullet holes, muddy trowsers, and leather scows, by courtesy called shoes, slit here and there to ease the chafe...."

CONNECTICUT

When Governor William Buckingham received the call for three regiments, he did not feel empowered to order out any of his eight existing regiments of Active Militia. Instead he requested a new organization of volunteers, composed of a combination of existing militia companies plus others newly formed. Some of these already wore their dark blue militia uniforms based on 1856 state regulations, which in turn were patterned on US Army regulations of 1851. According to the *Hartford Daily Courant* of April 20, others were uniformed by their local communities.

By the end of April the state's military authorities had also begun to supply uniforms to its volunteers. Major J.M. Hathaway, the State Quartermaster-General, contracted with firms in Hartford, Manchester and New Haven, CT, and in Monson, MA, to produce "coats, pantaloons, and blouses." One of the firms involved was clothier Charles Day of Hartford, who agreed to provide 500 "uniform coats" and 500 "pantaloons" at $7.50 per suit. Acquiring blue satinet cloth, he let the contract out to Hartford tailors who cut and made up the coats, and charged only for the latter. By the beginning of May, Day had agreed to supply 2,000 coats and 1,000 pairs of pantaloons, and was producing about 100 coats a day. On May 8 a correspondent of the Rhode Island *Providence Daily Evening Press* reported that Day also had orders for 2,000 overcoats, and had 13 cutters "constantly employed."

The uniforms worn by Connecticut troops arriving at the nation's capital were reported briefly in the Washington press. Commanded by Col (later Gen) Daniel Tyler, the 1st Connecticut were described in

Photographed at the studio of G.W. Davis in Hartford, this unidentified Connecticut volunteer wears an example of the dark blue uniform being produced in that city during April and May, 1861. His frock coat is trimmed around the base of the collar only, and his pants appear to be plain; he holds a chasseur-pattern cap. (Author's collection)

This volunteer from Hartford, CT, is tentatively identified as Wolcott P. Marsh, who enlisted in Rifle Company A, 1st Connecticut Infantry. He wears an example of the five-button coat with standing collar and breast pocket acquired by some Connecticut companies during the first few weeks of the war. (Author's collection)

the *Washington Star* of May 11 as wearing "blue frock coats, gray pants and fatigue caps." As with other states, much of the clothing issued to Connecticut volunteers was shoddily made. A report in the *Hartford Daily Courant* for May 20 stated that "seams ripped and buttons came off." Complaints from (among others) Capt Wright, commanding Co B, led to an investigation by a state legislative committee as early as the beginning of May 1861, which established that both gray and blue satinet had been acquired for trousers, and that the latter, made of "Reynolds satinet," had proved inferior. The trousers made up voluntarily by "the ladies of Hartford" for Charles Day were of inferior blue cloth.

DELAWARE

The second-smallest state in the Union, and one of four border or "slave states" that did not secede, Delaware was nevertheless reluctant to respond to the Presidential call for one regiment. Indeed, Democrat and pro-Southern Governor William Burton replied that there was "no organized militia in the State," and took no

The poor quality of the uniforms worn by these volunteers of the Delaware Blues (Co A, 1st Delaware Infantry) is apparent. Their coats are devoid of trim although they have a single small button attached either side of the collar. The man at right has a small metal letter "A" attached to the front of his cap. They are armed with M1842 muskets; shoulder belts support cartridge boxes, and 1839-pattern plates fasten their waist belts. (Military and Historical Imagebank)

active part in the formation of a regiment for the Union. However, Gen Henry Du Pont, a West Point graduate and senior partner in the largest gunpowder supplier to the Union Army during the Civil War, was nominally the State Adjutant-General, and he assumed leadership in the mobilization of Delaware militia.

The nucleus of the 1st Delaware Volunteer Militia was formed from the military companies in Wilmington, which included the Delaware Blues and Columbia Rifles. Volunteers enlisting from these units wore whatever uniform clothing they already had, whether full-dress or fatigue uniforms. Meanwhile the womenfolk organized a Volunteers' Sewing Society and made blue flannel shirts, blankets and haversacks for all the volunteer companies preparing for service. Attached to the command of Gen John Dix, Department of the Potomac, and assigned to duty guarding the line of the Philadelphia, Wilmington & Baltimore Railroad, Cos A, B, D and E, 1st Delaware, departed for duty without full uniforms on May 28, and the remainder of the regiment followed on June 9.

Still not supplied by June 2, a member of the Wilmington Rifles (Co E) reported in the *State Journal* from Camp Dare, by the Bush River, Maryland, that the "men begin to ask for their uniforms and overcoats." He also noted that havelocks had been received, and recorded a novel use for the flannel "body bandages" issued as a preventative for diarrhea, stating that "Some of the men wear the red flannel bands, designed for another part of the body, around their caps and on the outside of their garments, thus displaying a taste for martial colors not unbecoming a soldier."[4]

---

4   Throughout the 19th century it was erroneously believed in many armies that a flannel sash or body-belt worn under the coat would protect men from a variety of disorders and diseases, including dysentery and cholera. In fact their only real value was in providing support for the lower back if tightly wrapped.

With the exception of Companies H and I, on June 14–15 the 1st Delaware finally received poorly-made dark blue uniforms consisting of "coats, pantaloons, shoes, caps," and a member of the Wilmington Rifles reported in the *Delaware Republican* that the "boys" were "strutting about in their 'sojer' clothes." A letter of June 23 published in the *Philadelphia Inquirer* from Camp Milligan stated: "The men have received their uniforms; it is made of dark blue cassinet, with trimmings of light blue, making a very fine appearance when worn upon parades, drills or guard duties, being seldom worn at other times."

During the same period another volunteer wrote in the *Delaware Republican* of June 24 that "The long-looked for uniforms… are a pretty hard set of garments, very few fitting in anything like a decent manner, and reflecting but little credit on the tailor who cut them out. Some pants are too short, some too long, some too narrow in the waist, some too wide. – The coats have equally as many faults, some having no shape at all." By June 9 each company had received 32 "stout, durable" overcoats for use on guard duty, according to the *State Journal*.

Clearly not proud of his appearance, a member of the Sussex Volunteers (Co G) wrote in the *State Journal* on June 29: "Very little attention is paid to dress down here, there being no ladies to dress for. We are indifferent as to style; it is a matter of no moment whether we black our boots or not, or have on a collar, which we now regard as superfluous; we can wear our blue flannel shirts without either coat or vest, and have no apprehension of the ladies criticizing our appearance. We fit ourselves for the camp, not the parlor."

From a glass negative made by Jex J. Bardwell, this detail shows the 1st Michigan parading in the Campus Martius in Detroit to receive their regimental colors on May 1, 1861. As these volunteer militia companies had been brought together at such short notice they had yet to standardize their drill. Although they are all standing at "parade rest," the company at left is using the out-dated Scott's *Infantry Tactics* while the one at right is following Hardee's *Rifle and Light Infantry Tactics*. (Anne S.K. Brown Military Collection)

MICHIGAN

The single regiment required of Michigan was mustered-in at Fort Wayne, Detroit, on May 1, under Col Orlando B. Wilcox. Initially the money to equip the 1st Michigan was provided by the City of Detroit plus local businessmen and private citizens. By April 19, 1,600 blue flannel shirts had been made by Samuel Sykes & Co, with additional shirts, possibly of gray, being produced by local ladies' sewing societies. Meanwhile, according to the *Detroit Free Press* of April 30, Col Henry Whitlessey was sent east by Governor Austin Blair to purchase uniforms and camp equipment. Instead of acquiring uniforms, he bought about $20,000 worth of cloth sufficient for two regiments from A.T. Stewart & Co, a large dry-goods company in New York City; this consisted of "heavy Petersham blue [for] overcoats, navy blue lighter cloth for the fatigue jackets and pants, and blue flannel shirts."

Three leading Detroit merchant tailoring firms were contracted to make the uniforms. The jackets were plain, rather loose in cut, and fastened by nine buttons which were probably of the staff pattern embossed with the Michigan state seal, as this had been used by the state authorities since the 1840s. The standing collar had a seam at the top and a double line of welting around the center to make them stand upright, and cuffs were plain. Matching epaulets were secured by small gilt buttons near the collar. Many of the jackets had a single low-set slit pocket on the right side, between the sixth and seventh buttons. Although construction details of the dark blue flannel trousers are vague, they appear to have had a watch pocket on the right side and seam pockets on both sides. Non-commissioned officers' trousers lacked the customary seam stripes. On May 9, the *Detroit Free Press* advised that "the cloth for the pantaloons seems to be too thin, and the men will need to wear the drawers with which the exertions of the ladies of our city have supplied them." According to photographic evidence, the blue Petersham overcoats were of the caped infantry pattern as per 1851 US Army regulations, and headgear consisted of chasseur-pattern caps made by Buhl & Co of Detroit, who subcontracted the work to other hatters in the city.

Departing from Fort Wayne on May 13, the 1st Michigan represented the first Western troops to reach the Federal capital. Twelve days later it was ordered across the "Long Bridge" over the Potomac to take possession of Alexandria, Virginia. Following the establishment of Camp Wilcox, the uniforms of this regiment began to suffer from the extremes of campaign life. On June 23, Cpl J. Benton Kennedy (Co B) wrote to the *Jonesville Weekly Independent* that "Some of our boys are nearly bare-legged already, being furnished with but one pair of pants and one jacket very poorly made and of the slaziest [*sic*] kind of Navy flannel, which, in our rough life being obliged to wear them night and day, will last no time at all."

Fighting at Bull Run with the 2nd Brigade, Third Division commanded by Col Wilcox, the 1st Michigan formed part of the attack on the Confederate left flank. Involved in the struggle around the guns of Ricketts' Battery, this regiment advanced further into the Confederate lines than any other Union troops on July 21. As a result, it lost nine officers and 108 men killed, wounded and missing. When released during May 1862, one of those who had been captured stated in the *Detroit Free Press* that "the Michigan troops were known among the rebel soldiers as the 'blue jackets.' "

WISCONSIN

The single regiment requested of Governor Alex Randall from the "Far West" state of Wisconsin was designated the 1st Regiment, Wisconsin Active Militia. Rendezvousing at Milwaukee, it was mustered-in on May 19, finally leaving for the front on June 9. Based on reports in the *Milwaukee Daily Sentinel*, the state purchased "1,531½ yards gray cloth and 50 yards cadet cloth" from the Burlington Woolen Factory in Racine County before the end of April. This was made into 1,340 "gray woolen" coats and 1,218 pairs of trousers by at least 30 different Milwaukee tailors, the largest single order going to the Muller Brothers. At least 50 sets of coat and pants were produced by "about thirty convicts" with tailoring experience at the State Penitentiary. Also received were 817 caps and 1,645 flannel shirts.

Issued on May 6, these uniforms were ill-fitting and varied in color. In a letter written to the Fond du Lac *Reporter*, Pvt Colwert Pier stated that "We have just received our clothes, which they call uniforms, although one would think to see the company on parade, that the tailor had warranted each uniform to fit the largest man or the smallest boy. The cloth is gray, of various shades; much of it is of poor quality and will not stand hard service. The pants have a black cord down the sides, and the coats have brass buttons and stand-up collars."

Possibly due to dissatisfaction with the fit of their gray uniforms, the 1st Wisconsin also received blue fatigue clothing before they left the state, this consisting of 800 "overalls," and 868 "Blouses (Blue Denim)." However, the gray uniforms continued to be worn for dress occasions; while the regiment was en route through Illinois for Virginia the *Chicago Daily Tribune* of June 10 reported that it was dressed "all alike, frock coat and pants of dark gray cloth, with fatigue caps of the same."

The caps referred to were of képi style, trimmed around the band with black cord, and were of flimsy construction. Writing on May 22, an unknown volunteer stated in the *Milwaukee Morning Sentinel* that "The first night we got our caps we all hung them on our bayonets [on piled arms] to keep them out of the dirt, but in the morning we found that the fragile cloth had let the bayonets through, and the caps had slid down over the guns into the dirt." Two companies of the 1st Wisconsin eventually received new caps patterned on those worn by "the regular service," while the remainder of the regiment purchased replacements at their own expense.

During its three months of service the 1st Wisconsin campaigned in the Shenandoah Valley under Gen Robert Patterson, and fought at Falling Waters on July 2. Writing from Martinsburg, VA, nine days later, Pvt William Bird of the Madison Guards (Co E) stated in the *Wisconsin Daily Patriot* of July 17 that the Confederate infantry were uniformed "very similar to the Wisconsin men – so much so that we wear a white badge on our arm to designate us from them."

Members of the Milwaukee Light Guard (Co A, 1st Wisconsin), wearing uniforms made of cloth purchased from James Catlin at the Burlington Woolen Factory in Racine County. Their képi-style caps bear the metal letter "A" at front, and their lighter gray satinet nine-button frock coats have plain collar and cuffs. (Hoard Historical Museum, Fort Atkinson, Wisconsin)

IOWA

Commanded by Col J. Bates, the men of the 1st Iowa were mostly clothed in uniforms supplied by their local communities throughout their service, despite belated efforts by the state government to uniform them properly. In order to clothe the Governor's Greys and Jackson Guards of Dubuque, the tailors and cutters of that city provided their services free, and the Ladies' Volunteer Labor Society sewed the uniforms together by May 8. These uniforms finally reached the 1st Iowa via Mississippi River steamboat, following which *Dubuque Herald* correspondent F.B. Wilkie reported on May 12: "The coats and pantaloons fit magnificently and are admired as being the finest in the regiment. The boys have put on their uniforms, including their new hats – soft felt ones turned up on the left with a black, tasteful cockade." In the meantime, the rest of the 1st Iowa had received "Blankets, hats, stockings, shoes, &c." by May 6, while other companies also received uniforms from their hometowns. Recruited at Davenport, the German Rifles (Co G) wore "a light blouse with green collar and patent leather belt, dark gray pants without stripe except in the case of officers, a black felt [hat] turned up at one side and fastened by a tin bull's eye the size of a sauce plate, which displays the red, white and blue." According to the *Dubuque Herald* of May 5, the same general style was adopted by the Burlington and Mount Pleasant companies, although their blouses had "a profusion of bright red flannel trimmings."

Describing the process of clothing the Burlington Zouaves (Co E), Eugene Ware recalled: "Only about one-half... our company had uniforms, and being Zouave uniforms they were pronounced by our Mexican War veteran critics as unfit... so the girls... got up... a hunting-frock of the pioneer Daniel Boone type, fitting closely at the neck, cuff and belt... It was made of a fluffy, fuzzy, open-woven, azure-gray cloth... The cuff, collar and a band up and down the breast were flannel of a beautiful Venetian red, insuring a good target. Trowsers of a heavy buckskin type and color. Black felt hunting-hat, with a brilliant red-ribbon cockade... When we afterwards got into the field our officers made us tear off the red trimmings because they were too conspicuous."

MINNESOTA

The single regiment recruited in Minnesota was composed of ten of the existing militia companies. When the 1st Minnesota, commanded by Col Willis A. Gorman, passed through Chicago en route for Washington, DC, the *Chicago Daily Tribune* of June 24 observed: "Two hundred of these troops have the regular U.S. uniforms provided for U.S. infantry and supplied the volunteers at the forts. The balance wore blue shirts and red flannel shirts but will receive their uniforms at Harrisburg ordered thither from New York." When this regiment arrived at the Federal capital, the *National Daily Intelligencer* of June 28 confirmed that it had received a uniform consisting of "plain gray cassimere, trimmed with black, and a black felt hat, according to army regulations."

When they formed part of the 1st Brigade, Third Division at First Bull Run, the gray uniforms of the Minnesota troops confused both friend and foe during the fighting around Ricketts' Battery.

DISTRICT OF COLUMBIA

A total of eight provisional battalions of the militia were organized for service in the District of Columbia due to the efforts of Inspector-General Charles Stone, who did much to prevent pro-secessionist paramilitary groups from seizing the Federal capital. A composite 60-man company of the Washington Light Infantry Battalion was mustered-in on April 15, being the first Northern militia to enter active Federal service.

The companies composing the DC battalions wore uniforms of varying colors and cut. Some of the most striking included the gray frock coats and pants with orange facings, and glazed fatigue caps, of the Union Regiment, Co A, which formed part of the 2nd DC Battalion; the "gray pants, and coats with mixed red and orange facings, and gray fatigue caps with red tops," of the Washington Light Guard, 4th DC Battalion; and the "glazed fatigue cap, gray jacket with gold lace trimmings, and black pantaloons with gold stripe," of the Metropolitan Rifles, 5th DC Battalion.

Photographed in the Federal capital in April or May 1861, the two officers plus enlisted man dressed in gray (right) belong to District of Columbia militia companies, while the men at left are members of the 7th New York State Militia. (Anne S.K. Brown Military Collection)

SELECT BIBLIOGRAPHY

Officers and men of the Boston
Light Artillery, Massachusetts
Volunteer Militia, pose in front
of the Thomas Viaduct carrying
the Baltimore & Ohio Railroad.
Their undress caps are probably
dark blue, contrasting with their
gray double-breasted frock
coats. The enlisted men wear
brass shoulder scales, while
two officers (not wearing
epaulets) stand at the left.
Each man is armed with an
M1840 Light Artillery saber.
(Michael J. McAfee Collection)

Frederick H. Dyer, *Compendium of the War of the Rebellion* (1908)
Robert N. Scott, *Official Records of the War of the Rebellion* (Washington,
  DC, 1880–1901)
Reports of Committees of the House of Representatives... 1861–62, Vol. 2
  (Washington, DC, 1862)
http://Firtstbullrun.co.uk The Manassas Campaign, Virginia, 16-22
  July, 1861.

In state order, as on Contents page:
Samuel P. Bates, *History of Pennsylvania Volunteers, 1861–5* (Harrisburg,
  PA, 1869–71)
Frank H. Taylor, *Philadelphia in the Civil War* (Philadelphia, PA, 1913)
Adjutant-General, *Registers of New York in the War of the Rebellion, 1861
  to 1865* (Albany, NY, 1894–1906)
Correspondence to the Governor and Adjutant General, 1861–1866 – Series
  147–1A: 15 (Ohio Historical Society)
W.D. Allbeck, *Clark County Boys in Blue* (Springfield, OH, n.d.)
*Message and Reports to the General Assembly and Governor of the State of Ohio
  for the Year 1861* (Columbus, OH, 1862)
A.J. Grayson, *"The Spirit of 1861": History of the Sixth Indiana Regiment in
  the Three Months' Campaign in Western Virginia* (Madison, IN, 1875)
Indianapolis Directory & Business Mirror for 1861 (Indianapolis, IN, 1861)
*Diary of Thuma, Valentine (1839–?), Company K, 8th Indiana Volunteer
  Infantry* (Indiana Historical Society – SC 1458)
"Report of the [Indiana House] Select Committee to [I]nvestigate the
  Quartermaster and Commissary Department," in *Journal of the House
  of Representatives of the State of Indiana [Special Session Commencing...
  April 24, 1861]*, (Indianapolis, IN, 1861)

Lew Wallace, *Lew Wallace: an Autobiography*, Vol. 1 (New York, NY, 1906

Report of the Adjutant General containing Reports of the years 1861–66 (Springfield, MA, 1900–02)

Annual Report of the Quartermaster General of the State of New Jersey for the Year 1861 (Jersey City, NJ, 1862)

Robert Dollard, *Recollections of the Civil War and Going West to Grow Up in the Country* (Scotland, SD, 1906)

James A. Emmerton, *A Record of the Twenty-Third Regiment Mass. Vol. Infantry in the War of the Rebellion* (Boston, MA, 1886)

Maj John M. Gould & Rev Leonard G. Jordan, *History of the First – Tenth – Twenty-ninth Maine Regiment* (Portland, ME, 1871)

James O. Lyford, *History of Concord, New Hampshire* (City History Commission, 1896)

Thomas L. Livermore, *Days and Events,1860–1866* (Boston & New York, 1920)

Stephen G. Abbott, *The First Regiment New Hampshire Volunteers in the Great Rebellion* (Keene, NH, 1890)

Marcus Peladeau, "Green Mountain Soldiers: Vermonters in the Civil War," in *Military Images*, Vol. XIII, No. 2 (September–October 1991)

Augustus Woodbury, *Campaign of the First Rhode Island Regiment* (Providence, RI, 1862)

W.A. Croffut & John M. Morris, *History of Connecticut during the War of 1861–65* (New York, NY, 1869)

William P. Seville, *History of the First Regiment, Delaware Volunteers, from the commencement of the three months service to the final muster-out at the close of the Rebellion* (Wilmington, DE, 1884)

John Robertson (compiler), *Michigan in the War* (Lansing, MI, 1882)

Papers of the First Wisconsin, Series 1179 – Box 1 (Wisconsin Historical Society)

Eugene F. Ware, *The Lyon Campaign in Missouri. Being a History of the First Iowa Infantry* (Topeka, KS, 1907)

Records of the Columbia Historical Society, Vol. 28 (Washington, DC, 1926)

Plus various contemporary newspapers, as named in the text.

PLATE COMMENTARIES

A: PENNSYLVANIA

In the background is Ladner's Military Hall, a popular watering-hole for Pennsylvania militia in Philadelphia.

A1: Private, Sarsfield Rifles, 21st Pennsylvania Infantry

In full dress, this enlisted man shows off an 1851-pattern dress cap with dark green band and green "fountain" plume. His unusual "hunting-shirt"-style coat has a 2in-long fringe around the skirts. He is armed with a Model 1841 rifle, and his accoutrements consist of an 1839-pattern rifleman's powder flask and pouch, and a white buff leather 1839-pattern waist belt fastened with a small "US" oval plate.

A2: Musician, Philadelphia Zouave Corps, 1st Pennsylvania Infantry

Wearing the PZC uniform based on that of the Zouaves of the French Imperial Guard, the musician has a red fez with dark blue tassel, bound with a roll of white muslin resembling a turban. His blue jacket has yellow worsted "arabesque" trimmings and red cuffs, and his vest is similarly trimmed. A light blue sash is wrapped around his waist. His red pantaloons are tucked into leather leggings, over which are white gaiters or "greaves." His musician's belt has a drumstick holder at left and drum hook at right, plus supporting shoulder strap, mostly hidden here.

Also known as the "Howitzer Company," Co I, 12th New York State Militia was photographed at Camp Anderson, Washington, DC, in May 1861; compare with Plate B3. Most wear the chasseur uniform received by this regiment on May 9, and note the havelocks, top left. One of the regiment's 21 drummers, who wore zouave uniforms, sits in the right foreground, playing cards on the drumhead with his comrades. (Anne S.K. Brown Military Collection)

A3: Private, 2nd Pennsylvania Infantry (redesignated 19th Pennsylvania)

This rather poorly-dressed soldier wears a "Hardee" hat with full ornamentation, 1857-pattern four-button sack coat, red flannel shirt and plain sky-blue kersey trousers, and holds a black "pilot-cloth" infantry overcoat. He is armed with an M1842 Springfield musket, and his accoutrements (hidden here) consist of a black leather waist belt with oval "US" plate supporting a cap pouch and scabbarded bayonet. His 1842-pattern cartridge box is suspended from a black leather shoulder belt with a round "eagle" plate.

B: NEW YORK

B1: Private, Company A, 8th Regiment, New York State Militia (Washington Greys)

This soldier has been issued with the regulation undress uniform of his regiment: a cadet-gray cap with black band and regimental numeral, a four-button gray sack coat, and gray trousers with 2in-wide black seam stripes. He is fully equipped for the Bull Run campaign, and armed with an M1842 rifle-musket. The breast plate on his whitened buff shoulder belt displays a bust of George Washington within a wreath, and his waist belt a small rectangular brass plate bearing the company letter "A" with "WASHINGTON" in an arc above and "GREYS" below. The remainder of his accoutrements consist of a black leather cap pouch, bayonet scabbard, and cartridge box, plus an oilcloth haversack and tin drum canteen.

B2: Private, Company B, 13th NYSM (National Greys)

This company adopted a zouave-style uniform composed of a red fez with blue tassel; a light blue jacket with red cuffs, and white and yellow trim; a light blue vest with red and yellow trim; and red pantaloons tucked into white canvas leggings. He has a white waist belt secured by a plate showing the company letter "B" and "National/Greys," and black leather accoutrements for his M1842 Springfield musket.

The Irish nationalist Thomas Francis Meagher recruited the Irish Zouaves (Co K, 69th New York State Militia), whose uniform he wears here. Commissioned a brigadier general in 1862, he would command the Irish (2nd) Brigade, First Division, II Corps of the Army of the Potomac, which was decimated at Antietam and Fredericksburg in September and December 1862. After resigning his commission in May 1863, he was recalled to duty in September 1864, serving in the Western Theater. After briefly commanding a provisional division in the Army of the Ohio under Gen William T. Sherman, he finally resigned on May 15, 1865. (USAMHI)

B3: Private, 12th NYSM (Independence Guard)

Kneeling to adjust his canvas knapsack, this enlisted man wears the chasseur-style uniform received by his regiment on May 9, 1861: a "mazarine blue" fatigue cap with dark blue band and the brass regimental number; a dark blue coat trimmed with light blue; and sky-blue pantaloons tucked into russet leather leggings. He carries an M1855 rifle-musket, and has black leather accoutrements and a white blanket roll. A large red, white and blue Union rosette is pinned to his coat.

C: OHIO, INDIANA, & ILLINOIS

C1: NCO, 19th Ohio Volunteer Infantry

The shoddily dressed NCO wears a dark blue 1858-pattern forage cap, plain gray nine-button jacket, and matching pants with broad black seam stripes. He is armed with an imported Enfield rifle-musket, and accoutrements include a black leather belt fastened with an oval "OVM" plate, plus a tin drum canteen and oilcloth haversack.

C2: Private, Company K, 16th Ohio (Springfield Greys)

This volunteer wears a similarly poor-quality uniform, consisting of a red flannel shirt supplied by his state, plain gray trousers, and an 1861-pattern forage cap with lower crown and oilskin cover. He holds a Liége-made French M1857 rifle-musket and has black leather accoutrements; note the 1858-pattern "clamshell"-shaped canteen with gray cloth cover.

C3: Private, 9th Indiana Infantry

Outfitted in a plain jacket and pants of blue jean cloth, with a broad-brimmed hat pinned up (with a military button and red worsted cord), this enlisted man carries an M1855 rifle-musket and has an 1855-pattern cartridge box; his equipage includes a tin canteen in a pale blue cover.

C4: Private, 12th Illinois Volunteers (The First Scotch Regiment)

The "tam-o'-shanter"-style cap with a shallow plaid band indicates the Scottish nucleus of this regiment. The remainder of his uniform consists of a seven-button gray coat, with three small buttons along a narrow strip of cloth on the cuffs. Recruited in Chicago, this regiment was issued M1857 Württemberg rifle-muskets and black leather accoutrements, with white cotton haversacks.

D: NEW JERSEY & MASSACHUSETTS

D1: Private, 1st New Jersey Foot Militia

He wears the state uniform supplied to its three-month militia: a dark blue forage cap and frock coat, with white trim around the base of the collar, the cuffs and the "bridle" or epaulet

Photographed at Washington, DC, three of these enlisted men of the 8th Massachusetts Volunteer Militia wear Federal-issue clothing and caps, which were probably part of the uniform issued to the regiment by special order of Abraham Lincoln on May 17, 1861. However, the left-hand man wears the full-dress gray uniform of the Allen Guard (Co K), formed in Pittsfield, MA, in August 1860 – compare with the similar uniform worn by Plate D2. Before reorganization in April 1861, the Allen Guard was Co A, 1st Battalion of Infantry, MVM, hence the letter "A" still attached to his cap front. (Anne S.K. Brown Military Collection)

Standing at "Order arms" with M1842 smoothbore percussion muskets, these unidentified enlisted men of the 1st New Hampshire show to good effect the cadet-gray uniforms made in Boston, MA, by Whiting, Galloupe, Bliss & Co, and Whitten, Hopkins & Co. Indicating a lack of uniformity, the coat worn by the man at the left lacks any of the red trim just visible on his comrade's collar and cuffs. (Courtesy Ron Swanson)

straps, plus sky-blue pants with narrow white seam stripes. He has an M1842 rifle-musket and appropriate accoutrements and field equipment, including a black rubberized canvas knapsack and a white cotton haversack.

D2: Private, Company C, 6th Massachusetts Volunteer Militia (Mechanic Phalanx)

Numerous Massachusetts companies had a dress uniform composed of a nine-button gray tailcoat and matching pants, with variously colored trim across the chest. That of the Mechanic Phalanx was trimmed with yellow, and had the same color facings on collar and cuffs plus a yellow band on their gray fatigue caps. He is armed with an M1842 rifle-musket, and accoutrements include a whitened leather shoulder belt and black waist belt, a combination worn by many MVM units.

D3: Private, 3rd Massachusetts Volunteer Militia

The odd-looking headgear is the hat designed by Gen B.F. Edmands, an MVM officer, which was buttoned up on all four sides and trimmed with red. His seven-button gray "chasseur"-style jacket is also trimmed with red around the collar only. He holds an M1855 rifle-musket, and is showing off a private-purchase M1849 Colt Pocket revolver.

E: MAINE, NEW HAMPSHIRE, & DISTRICT OF COLUMBIA

The incomplete Capitol dome in Washington, DC, is seen in the background.

E1: Private, 1st Maine Volunteer Militia

This volunteer wears a plain gray 1858-pattern forage cap. The unit's seven-button gray frock coat, with tall, square-cut standing collar, was reportedly of very poor quality cloth, and the plain gray pants were made from shoddy material showing a mixture of red and brown flecks. His black waist belt is fastened with a small version of the 1839-pattern oval "US" plate, and supports an 1828-pattern scabbarded bayonet and a black leather cap pouch for his M1855 Springfield rifle-musket.

E2: Private, 1st New Hampshire Volunteers, full dress

This enlisted man wears the full-dress uniform supplied by New Hampshire for its regiment of three-month volunteers. It consisted of a cadet-gray tail coat and pants, with red trim which varied in detail between the companies. The cadet-gray chasseur-pattern cap had a red band, and a state button fastened at the front. Supplementing his M1842 smoothbore percussion musket, he too has an 1849 Colt Pocket revolver tucked in his belt.

E3: Private, 1st New Hampshire Volunteers, fatigue dress

Many militia units had full-dress uniforms but lacked fatigue clothing suitable for active service in the field. When this regiment was mobilized the troops were additionally issued with blue "sack" coats for fatigue dress; this is the uniform they wore at First Bull Run.

E4: Private, Company E, 4th Battalion, District of Columbia Militia (Washington Zouaves)

This company's blue jackets were edged with buff trim and had brass "bell" buttons, worn over a "tea-green" shirt with yellow trim and white bone buttons on the front. Light blue pantaloons with buff seam stripes were tucked into leather leggings. The weapon was the M1855 rifle-musket.

F: RHODE ISLAND & CONNECTICUT

In the background are the wooden barracks of Camp Sprague in Washington, DC.

F1: Officer, 1st Rhode Island Detached Militia

This officer has a more elaborate version of the blue "hunting-shirt" worn by his regiment, which has a broad falling collar, and six pleats either side of an eight-button single-breasted front. His hat bears a black ostrich-feather plume, and is pinned up at the right with an 1858-pattern "eagle" plate. The trousers are plain gray. He holds an M1850 foot officers' sword, and has a holstered M1851 Colt Navy revolver on his belt.

F2: Kady Brownell, attached 1st Rhode Island Detached Militia

One of at least three "vivandiéres" known to have been attached to this regiment, she wears a black hat with a black ostrich-feather plume, the brim pinned up with a large white embroidered star. Around her neck is a white silk stock with a Rhode Island state button attached at the front. Her blue blouse with two rows of small brass buttons is tucked into a red skirt, worn over loose-cut gray trousers gathered to the ankles. She has a white waist sash with gold fringes; under this a waist belt supports a militia dress sword in a black leather scabbard. Note also her buckskin gauntlets, and ankle-high black bootees.

F3: Private, 1st Connecticut Volunteers

Holding an M1859 Sharps rifle with sword-bayonet at the "Shoulder arms," this volunteer wears a plain dark blue forage cap, a nine-button frock coat with sky-blue trim around the base of the collar, and plain dark blue pants.

F4: Private, Company A, 1st Connecticut Volunteers

For fatigue dress this regiment received a plain gray four-button sack coat with standing collar and an open pocket on the left chest. He also wears a white cotton havelock, popular with many three-month regiments, in this case with the corners buttoned together beneath the chin. His equipage includes a combined canteen/ration box instead of a canteen and haversack; painted medium blue, it is marked "Compy A" and "Conn Volunteers."

G: MICHIGAN, WISCONSIN, & VERMONT

G1: Private, 1st Michigan Volunteers

Holding an M1855 rifle-musket at "Charge – bayonet" to defend against infantry attack, he wears a dark blue chasseur-pattern cap, a nine-button jacket with epaulet or "bridle" straps and a single low-set slit pocket in the right side, plus matching pants. A red, white and blue Union cockade is fastened to his chest. Note his canteen, with a red cloth cover.

G2: Corporal, Company A, 1st Wisconsin Volunteers (Milwaukee Light Guard)

Armed with an M1842 rifle-musket, he is conspicuous in his nine-button frock coat of light gray satinet, worn with a cadet-gray chasseur-style cap trimmed with black cord, and plain dark gray pants.

G3: Private, 1st Vermont Volunteers

This Vermont enlisted man, armed with an M1861 Springfield rifle-musket, wears a cadet-gray forage cap with a sprig of green leaves attached; a cadet-gray tail coat fastened with nine state seal buttons, with black epaulet straps; and much-repaired pants of the same color, with black side stripes. (Some Union three-month volunteers deliberately made a display of large, colorful patches on their trousers, to advertise their contempt for the profiteering suppliers of shoddy clothing.)

The variety of uniforms worn on this plate reminds us of the notorious episodes of confusion between friend and foe that occurred during the first clashes of the war, when gray-clad Union troops confronted Confederates in blue uniforms.

H: DELAWARE, MINNESOTA, & IOWA

H1: Private, 1st Delaware Volunteer Militia

Armed with an M1842 smoothbore musket, and dressed in a poorly-made dark blue frock coat trimmed with sky-blue around the collar only, with a single small button on each side of the same, this enlisted man has attempted to give himself a more colorful appearance by adding to his tall, old-fashioned forage cap a strip of the red flannel abdominal "bandage" or belly band, issued in the belief that keeping the stomach warm was a preventative against diarrhea.

H2: Private, 1st Minnesota Volunteers

Uniformed as he appeared on departure from his home state, he wears a black felt hat pinned up with an "eagle" plate and bearing an infantry buglehorn front badge; a plastron-fronted red flannel shirt; and plain dark blue pants. He too is armed with a smoothbore musket, and carries a Bowie knife with a German-silver handle at his belt.

H3: Private, Company G, 1st Iowa Infantry (German Rifles)

The womenfolk of Davenport, Iowa, made the uniform worn by this volunteer of a German immigrant community: a light gray five-button sack coat with a dark green standing collar, and plain dark gray pants. His black felt hat is turned up on the left, with a cockade described as "a tin bull's eye the size of a sauce plate, which displays the red, white and blue." Besides an M1816 musket converted from flintlock to percussion, he has an M1848 Colt Baby Dragoon revolver. His black patent leather waist belt is fastened by a militia "eagle" plate, and supports the usual black leather cap pouch and bayonet scabbard.

INDEX

References to illustrations are shown in **bold**.
Captions to plates are shown in brackets.

Abbott, Joseph 24
Andrew, John 20

Bates, Col J. 40
blankets 35
body bandages **H1**(32, 47), 36
Boston Light Artillery **42**
Brown, James M. 12
Brownell, Kady **F2**(30, 47)
Buckingham, William 35
Burnside, Ambrose 34, 35
Burton, William 36
Butler, Gen Benjamin 33

Cairo Expedition, the 16
Call to Arms 3–4
Cameron, Simon 34
cartridge boxes **A3**(25, 44), **C3**(27, 45), 13, 36
cavalry 3, 6
Chicago 16, 16–17
chronology 4–5
coats **A3**(25, 44), **F3**(30, 47), **3**, 7, 9, **9**, 10, 11, 13, **16**, **17**, 20, **21**, 22, **22**, 23, 24, 35, **35**, **36**
Connecticut **F3–4**(30, 47), 3, 5, **35**, 35–6
Corwine, Maj R. 12

Day, Charles 35
Delaware **H1**(32, 47), 3, 5, **36**, 36–7
District of Columbia **E4**(29, 46), 3, 5, 41, **41**
drummers **44**
Du Pont, Gen Henry 36

Fairbanks, Erastus 33
fatigue dress **E3**(29, 46), **F4**(30, 47), 9, **9**, **10**, 10, 11, 16, **19**, 34
First Bull Run (Manassas) campaign 4–5, 5, 10, 38, 40

Goodwin, Ichabod 23

Hale, Reuben C. 6
Hathaway, Major J.M. 35
headgear 12, **14**, 15, 17–18, 34, 39
caps 3, 7, 9, 10, **11**, 13, 14, **19**, **20**
chasseur-pattern **G2**(31, 47), 24, **24**, 38
the Edmands hat **D3**(28, 46), **21**, 21
Hardee hat **A3**(25, 44)
Havelock Cap 17–18, 33, **44**
Kossuth hat 11, 34
straw hats 19
tam-o'-shanter-style **C4**(27, 45), **16**, 17
zouave **B2**(26, 44), 10, 11, 17
huntingshirt coats **A1**(25, 44), **6**
hunting-shirts **F1**(30, 47), 34, **34**

Illinois **C4**(27, 45), 3, 5, **16**, 16–18, **17**
Indiana **C3**(27, 45), 3, 5, **14**, 14–15, **15**
Iowa **H3**(32, 47), 3, 5, 40

jackets **D3**(28, 46), **10**, 13, 14, **16**, **18**, **20**, 38, 46

Ladd, Luther **3**
Lincoln, Abraham 3–4
Loomis, James M. 17–18

Maine **E1**(29, 46), 3, 5, **22**, 22–3
Massachusetts **D2–3**(28, 46), **3**, 3, 5, 19, 19–20, **20**, **21**, **42**, **45**

Meagher, Thomas Francis **44**
Michigan **G1**(31, 47), 3, 5, **37**, 38
militia box-knapsacks **9**
Minnesota **H2**(32, 47), 3, 40
Morris, T. 14
Morton, Oliver 14
musicians **A2**(25, 44)

Neal, Charles "Bucky" 8
New Hampshire **E2–3**(29, 46), 3, 5, **23**, 23–4, **24**, **46**
New Jersey **D1**(28, 45–46), 3, 5, **18**, 18–19
New York **B**(26, 44–45), **3**, **4**, 5, 8, **9**, 9–11, **10**, **11**, 17, **41**, **44**
non-commissioned officers **C2**(27, 45), **G2**(31, 47), **7**, **10**, **20**, 38

officers **41**, **42**
Ohio **C1–2**(27, 45), 3, 5, **11**, 11–14, **12**, **13**
Olden, Charles 18

Patterson, Gen Robert 39
Pennsylvania **A**(25, 44), 3, 5, **6**, 6–8, **7**
Phelps, John 33
Philadelphia 6, **6**, **7**
Platt, William 12
profiteers 8

Randall, Alex 39
Reed, John 21
regimental organization 3
regiments
1st Connecticut **F3–4**(30, 47), **35**
1st Delaware **H1**(32, 47), **36**, 36–7
1st Iowa Infantry **H3**(32, 47), 40
1st Maine Volunteer Militia **E1**(29, 46), **22**, 22–3
1st Michigan Volunteers **G1**(31, 47), **37**, 38
1st Minnesota Volunteers **H2**(32, 47), 40
1st New Hampshire Volunteers **E2–3**(29, 46), **24**, 24, **46**
1st New Jersey Foot Militia **D1**(28, 45–46), 18
1st Ohio Volunteer Infantry **11**, 11–12
1st Pennsylvania Infantry **A2**(25, 44)
1st Regiment, Detached Militia **34**, 34–5
1st Rhode Island Detached Militia **F1–2**(30, 47)
1st Vermont Volunteers **G3**(31, 47), 33
1st Wisconsin Volunteers **G2**(31, 47), 39, **39**
2nd Maine Volunteers 23
2nd New Jersey Foot Militia 19
2nd Ohio Volunteer Infantry 11–12
2nd Pennsylvania Infantry **A3**(25, 44)
3rd Massachusetts Volunteer Militia **D3**(28, 46), 19, 21
3rd New Jersey Foot Militia 19
4th Massachusetts Volunteer Militia 19, 20, 21, **21**
4th New Jersey Foot Militia **17**, 18, 19
5th Massachusetts Volunteer Militia 19, 20
5th New York State Militia (NYSM) 9
6th Indiana 14, 15
6th Massachusetts Volunteer Militia **D2**(28, 46), **3**, 19, 20, 21
6th New York State Militia 9
7th Illinois 16, **16**
7th New York State Militia **4**, 9, **9**, 17, **41**
8th Indiana Infantry 14–15, 15
8th Massachusetts Volunteer Militia 19, **19**, **20**, **44**
8th New York State Militia **B1**(26, 44), **9**, 9
9th Illinois 17

9th Indiana Infantry **C3**(27, 45), 15
10th Illinois 18
10th Indiana Infantry **14**, 15
11th Illinois 18
11th Indiana **15**, 15
12th Illinois Volunteers **C4**(27, 45), **16**, 17
12th New York State Militia 10, **44**
13th New York State Militia **B2–3**(26, 44–45), 10, **10**, **11**
14th Ohio Volunteer Infantry 13, 15
15th Ohio Volunteer Infantry 13
16th Ohio Volunteer Infantry **C2**(27, 45), 13
17th Ohio Volunteer Infantry 12, 13–14
18th Ohio Volunteer Infantry 13
19th Ohio Volunteer Infantry **C1**(27, 45), 13
19th Pennsylvania Infantry **7**, 7–8
20th New York State Militia 11
20th Ohio Volunteer Infantry 13
21st Pennsylvania Infantry **A1**(25, 44), **6**
25th New York State Militia 11
25th Pennsylvania 6, 7
28th New York State Militia 10
34th Ohio Volunteer Infantry 21
69th New York State Militia 10–11, **44**
71st New York State Militia 11
Rhode Island **F1–2**(30, 47), 3, 5, **34**, 34–5

service 5
Shenandoah Valley campaign 4, 39
shirts 7, 13, 14, 20, 22
Sprague, William 34
state quotas 3, 6, 14, 18, 19, 22, 23
Swift, BrigGen Richard 16

terms of service 3
trousers **F1**(30, 47), **3**, 7, 9, **10**, 10, 11, 13, 14, **16**, **17**, **19**, 24, **33**, 35, 38

uniforms 6
color 7, 10, 11, 14, 15, 20, 21, 22, 33, 39, 41
cost 14, 24, 34, 35
full dress **A1**(25, 44), **E2**(29, 46), **3**, **4**, **44**
gray **B1**(26, 44), **D3**(28, 46), **E1–2**(29, 46), **G2–3**(31, 47), **H3**(32, 47), **7**, 7, **9**, 9, 10, 11, **13**, 13–14, **15**, 15, **16**, 16, 17, 20, 21, **21**, 22, **22**, 23–4, **24**, 33, **33**, 39, **39**, 40, **41**, 41, **44**, **46**
procurement 6–8, 12, 16, 16–17, 23, 35
quality **C1–2**(27, 45), 7–8, **8**, 12, 13–14, 14–15, 18, 20, 23, 24, 33, 35, **36**, 36, 38, 39
US Army 3, 9

Vermont 3, **G3**(31, 47), 5, **33**, 33
vivandiéres **F2**(30, 47)

Wallace, Col Lew **15**, 15
weapons
muskets **A3**(25, 44), **B2**(26, 44), **H**(32, 47), 6, **9**, 13, 16, **36**, 46
personal sidearms **E2**(29, 46), **F1**(30, 47), **H3**(32, 47), 12, **23**
rifle-muskets **B1**(26, 44), **B3**(26, 45), **C**(27, 45), **D**(28, 46), **E4**(29, 46), **G**(31, 47), 33
sabres **42**
Sharps rifle **F3**(30, 47)
Western Virginia campaign 4
Wilcox, Col Orlando B. 38
Wisconsin **G2**(31, 47), 3, 5, **39**, 39

zouaves and zouave uniform **A2**(25, 44), **B2**(26, 44), 6, 10, 10–11, **11**, **15**, 15, 17, **18**, 19, 40